To my wife, Nati. Thank you for your love, positivity, and support.

To my parents, for being the best role models in life and work.

To Aamen, my co-founder for always coming in clutch.

ORIGINAL SERIES

ORIGINAL SERIES:

How to create binge-worthy,
B2B content that drives revenue

Kareem Mostafa

Icon design by Freepik from www.flaticon.com

First Edition

ISBN: 978-1-08934-116-1

Independently published

Table of Contents

Foreword by Chris Savage, CEO at Wistia

Online marketing is getting harder and harder every day.

It wasn't always this hard. Before the entire world started doing it, you could get decent results just writing useful posts for your blog or running ads for your Facebook page.

Today, those channels are too crowded. There are more than 60 million business pages on Facebook alone. Some estimates say there are more than 500 million blogs on the internet, with two new posts being published every second.

Because of the amount of noise out there, the old playbooks don't work the same way— and tactics we once used are no longer a competitive advantage.

Today, between Amazon, Netflix, Hulu and all the other options out there, people have a virtually endless supply of high-quality *and* free (or cheap) content available at the touch of a button.

To stand out in a world full of noise and unlimited distractions, marketers need to focus on building strong brands, not grinding out impressions and gaming their audience for clicks.

Digital advertising is a great tool for businesses. But digital advertising alone won't make people like you. You can't build trust, affinity, and advocacy with tools designed to optimize your conversion rates and grind out impressions. You don't show people you have clear values and a brand they should care about by forcing your advertisements on them on social media.

Yet over the last decade, Google and Facebook have become the online marketing channels of choice for a vast number of businesses across industries. And while a handful have been successful picking low-hanging fruit, most are left scrambling and competing for crumbs.

Digital advertising today is an arms race with diminishing returns. There are more companies than ever vying for the attention of people who have never been more occupied with other forms of media. If you want different results—if you really want people to care—you need to try something different.

You need to build a brand.

The biggest untruth inflicted upon marketers in the last several years is the idea that brand is a nebulous, feel-good buzzword.

The truth is that building affinity is relatively straightforward. Traditionally, brand affinity comes from all the interactions with your product: what it feels like to use your product, what support, sales and success experiences feel like, and your website. An amazing experience for your customers will turn them into advocates, and advocates will share and propagate your message.

But how does marketing create brand affinity? You need people to spend time with your brand. You need them to have a personal connection. The best way to do that is to make long-form content that is unique, that resonates with their core values, and that makes them *want* to come back to you time and time again.

More than a decade ago, Seth Godin coined the term "permission marketing," the idea being that your marketing should be so valuable that people feel like they missed out when they don't get an email from you.

Today, it's about building content that people actively seek out when they're not hearing from you. It's about building content that adds real value rather than pushing people along towards the next stage in the funnel. It's about creating something that is so focused on the niche of your best customers, that for them your content can compete with the likes of *Game of Thrones* and Netflix for their attention.

This kind of thinking only used to make sense for media companies and big brands with huge budgets, but that's changed. You don't need an HBO-sized budget anymore to start making addictive, binge-worthy, and valuable content for your niche, whether that's buyers of back-end SaaS for dentist offices, lovers of old restored guitars, or startup and SMB video marketers.

In this book, you'll learn the art and science of creating binge-worthy content, from the different types of content you can create and how to craft a competitive advantage, to how you should be thinking about distribution and building internal consensus around content on your team.

It's more critical than ever that businesses start embracing this way of thinking. If you want to cut through the noise, build loyalty among your customers, and get them to talk about your brand with their friends, then this book is for you.

Enjoy.

- Chris Savage. CEO at Wistia

Introduction

Fellow B2B marketers and business owners:

I like to think that you're probably reading this book because you're in need of a much-needed break.

I'm sitting in my office as I write this introduction. In 0.68 seconds, Google returned 2,140,000,000 results when I searched for "content marketing strategy".

If you're a small business owner, you may be thinking of ways to grow your company's brand and sales predictably, in order to establish yourself in the market and safeguard yourself against growing costs. Maybe you've been reading a lot about various marketing strategies and sales processes and unsure where to start. Or it may be possible that you've already tried your hand at creating some content but it fell on deaf ears. You're in the right place.

If you're the CMO, VP, or director at a larger company - you may be concerned with keeping up to date with the latest trends and best practices in marketing to improve sales and marketing alignment while cementing your company's thought leadership in new and existing domains. Perhaps what used to work no longer works as effectively as before, despite experimenting with different content approaches. You're in the right place too.

If you're a content marketer, you may be experiencing burnout due to all the elements that need to come together for your content efforts to pay off. You may still be fending off others around you who are still questioning the power of content to grow a business. Maybe you're just fatigued by the sheer volume of content out there on how to create content, or marketing and business growth strategies in general. Or maybe it's the lead time. The back and forth. All the editing that goes into just getting one content piece over the line.

If you're a social selling rep or sales leader, you may be starting to recognize that content is "everyone's" job - and that it can fast track your success to build personal brands and engage with prospects and target accounts with relevant content long before going in for the ask, but will creating content take from your sales productivity? Besides - what's the guarantee any of this will work?

Disclaimer: Throughout the book, I will refer to 'marketers' most of the time, though this term should not exclude any person's role in B2B involved with marketing a brand, product or service in some form. This includes, business owners, senior leadership, salespeople, among others.

It's real out there.
In one way shape or form, content is important to all of us - regardless of what our role is in our brands. What happens when everyone starts to do content though? What happens

when everyone has videos, blogs, or image content? How do we continue to stand out?

Imagine your brand creating something so remarkable that it would be near impossible to replicate exactly, and not only make the competition irrelevant but will continue to safeguard you as you build on top of it and cement your brand and revenue generation efforts.

By reading this book and applying the principles in it, you will put an end to the question of "what should our content strategy be?". More fundamentally, it will change the way you see all the content around you. It will help you gain clarity on what's *really* going on. It will help you rise one level above the current status quo that you see all around you so that you can make a few key - almost nuanced - moves that have huge bottom line impacts that can be quantitatively measured.

It will help you begin to create content that runs in an integrated, seamless fashion - as opposed to departmental silos. Most famously - it will naturally compound your marketing and sales efforts to generate more traffic, better quality leads, and shorter lead times.

This is the story of how some clever brands have tipped the scales in their favour by creating original series to grow results from content marketing exponentially, and how they did it. They created episodes which then got repurposed into multitudes of content pieces across video, audio, written, and image.

Think of this book not as an encyclopedia, but as an "essentials handbook" designed to live quietly on your desk for when inspiration strikes. In this book you and I will go on a journey to get re-introduced to content marketing, understand where it all changed, and how a new wave of brands are redefining the content game as we know it and growing their brands while everyone binge-watches their content. Most importantly, we will talk about how you can replicate that for your own brand.

Specifically, we will cover the benefits of creating original series, and how brands can plan, execute, measure, and scale their original series productions. It also makes reporting on revenue results easier and more systematic.

It's not only more fun and less stress, it's more meaningful work. Creating meaningful, impactful work is our north star after all; it's the original reason why we all chose to do what we do.

I hope you enjoy this book and that it sparks the right conversations with you and your team.

Let's jump right in.

- Kareem

PART I:

= *"When the student is ready, the master appears."*

– Buddhist Proverb

1. Content Marketing: A Re-introduction

1a. The Change in the Modern Buyer's Journey

It was a good day [in Dublin].
I'm from Egypt, where it's always sunny weather, but we don't really think much of it. In fact, we hate how hot it can get and always seek shade wherever we can. When I moved to Ireland eight years ago all of that changed. I began to cherish sunny weather. It's not always sunny here, and so when the sun comes out you learn to appreciate it and make the most of it. This includes leaving work early, calling in sick (sorry boss), having outdoor meetings, eating ice cream - or throwing instant BBQs when the weekend comes around. Besides, it's always just the right amount of sunny. Never too hot. Definitely not. I digress.

It was a particularly beautiful, sunny Saturday morning in Dublin and I was in the market for a new camera. Usually, I'd do my usual Amazon and Google research and get sorted, but the old soul in me decided to make use of the sun and visit a local camera shop in the city center.

I had already researched a little bit online, and hadn't made a decision yet. I walked into the shop, and was met with a friendly older gentleman, who guided me through different cameras within my price range - ultimately recommending one particular one. I had read about that camera before and had some concerns about it, but he assured me that they are insignificant. I left convinced that this is the camera for me.

Later that day, I returned home and went online. I was prepared to purchase that camera, but a few days later, after doing more online research about the flaws that the shopkeeper dismissed, I decided that the camera was a no-go for me.

A few YouTube tech review videos and articles later, I fell in love with another camera and ended up going for that one. It seemed my old habits have trumped going into a shop and buying based on over-the-counter advice. I found so much content online that made me feel confident in my decision.

I felt, even if for a few days, like a camera expert. Having read and watched tens of hours of content to help me arrive at my decision, I even started recommending that camera to others in my circle, like a self-proclaimed camera guru that I'm not.

New, Old Habits

Do you remember the rush of going into an electronics store to find a new laptop to buy? Cue the warm greeting from the friendly sales clerk, who then offers their expertise as they guide you straight down the catwalk of shiny computers they have on sale in their store, right down to one specific one that just happens to fit our budget range.

With blind faith, and somewhat starstruck, we nod, take their recommendation and make the purchase then and there. Yup, that was a long time ago. There was nothing wrong with it, just that the internet and mobile phones changed everyone's habits. Our new habits have become our old habits, our old ways - for buying.

Today, people go computer shopping armed with the equivalent of a PhD on the products they're in the market for, regardless of whether they buy online or offline.

They've read blogs, watched videos, and were probably fit to sit an exam on feature comparison at this stage. Except it's not just computers, it's most anything and everything in commerce. The buyer's journey has changed drastically in the last decade.

Quick! Act like an influencer

The other day my wife and I went to one of our favourite Italian restaurants for some pizza and pasta in a local neighbourhood not too far from where we live. While waiting for our starters to arrive, we were super occupied with the camera I had on me which I recently purchased. Pushing all the buttons, trying all the settings. You would've thought we're two [wannabe] influencers vlogging about the restaurant, though sadly we got no preferential treatment whatsoever. Our waitress served our starters and enquired what camera that was as she came closer to take a look.

"Nice camera. I'm going to Japan soon and I'm looking for a good portable one."

I mumbled the name of the camera in between bites, and she said thanks and left us to it. I felt that she only politely said thanks but didn't fully catch the name of the camera as she darted off. When we were leaving, I offered to write it down on a piece of paper for her in case she wanted to get the exact name of the model (it was a Sony a5100 mirrorless). She said, "Oh I know that camera well, it came up in my research when I was searching for cameras online that perform well in low-light conditions."

Was she a fellow "camera expert" too?

As she continued to tell me more features about my own camera, I refrained from dropping my jaw. Keep in mind we both (or at least I) never worked in the camera industry before.

Have you ever been in a situation where you knew more about a product than the person selling it?

This happens all the time.

People become overnight insiders in different topics based on what they're in the market for. No need to consult with an expert, or a sales clerk. It is likely you may end up knowing more about the product or service than them, at least in the context of your own needs. You have the leverage of insight gathered from online reviews, detailed video walkthroughs, articles, influencer opinions, and so on. You literally *studied* this stuff.

All the information needed is available at our fingertips on Google, YouTube, Amazon, and social media.

In fact, according to Sirius Decisions, at least 67% of today's buyer journey is done online. In his book *To*

Sell is Human, Daniel Pink refers to it as the shift from the old *caveat emptor* (buyer beware) world to the now-contemporary *caveat venditor* (seller beware) state of affairs. In other words, the buyer has all the power today, because of access to unlimited information online. This leaves marketers and salespeople in a bit of a pickle.

It's all about the journey

brands that most get ahead in today's world are the ones that make it as easy as possible for their customers to buy whenever and however. They understand that there are three different types of people who can buy from them at any given time, and because they think different, they also search differently. This gives us the buyer's journey. The buyer's journey is at the core of the Inbound Marketing Methodology (popularised by Hubspot), by which brands attract, engage, and delight their customers. Here's a breakdown of each stage of the buyer's journey.

1. Awareness
2. Consideration
3. Decision

1. Awareness:

In the awareness stage, people begin experiencing the very first symptoms of the challenge they wish to address or goal they wish to attain and begin initial research to familiarise themselves better with it. During this time, they don't know what they don't know and are just trying to get to grips with the topic as a whole before diving deeper.

Search Examples:
The best camera to take on a trip
Ways to make passive income
How to build muscle fast

2. Consideration:

Having done some initial research, they are now more familiar with the different options to go about their solution strategy. In the consideration stage, their research is focused on comparing different alternatives, collecting additional information on the pros and cons of various potential solutions to their challenge or goal.

Search Examples:
DSLR vs GoPro cameras for traveling
Are index funds better than stocks
What's better gym or home workouts

3. Decision:

Having understood their goal much better and familiarize themselves with the different options available to them, the decision stage is focused on deciding between different brands or vendors to go with. During this time, they narrow down by looking at features and benefits, testimonials, and case studies as they finalize picking one over the other to solve their challenge.

Examples:
Canon G7x Mark II vs Sony a5100
Where to buy S&P 500 Index
Rock climbing gym near me

brands use the buyer's journey as a framework to align themselves to their buyers' way of thinking, striving to provide them with the right resources (i.e: content) at the right time. Whereas traditional B2B marketers and salespeople focus solely on the *decision* stage, modern B2B brands understand the long game, and that it is important for them to create content addressing their buyers' questions to help guide their thought process throughout their journey.

This way of thinking in itself was a breakthrough to many brands, who felt that their time should be primarily focused on creating online and offline collateral to promote the features, benefits, and even customer testimonials of their products and services.

While this [decision stage] is important, it arguably represents the final third of the buyer's journey and what is really going on in buyers' minds. Not to mention, the decision stage is the one that comes easiest to brands, it is naturally the most competitive.

If we type in any decision-stage queries in Google Search, we will find that it is overpopulated with ads - which is one key indicator that a certain keyword is competitive and in demand. Besides, who likes being sold to? Brands that build top of the funnel (TOFU) content and bottom of the funnel (BOFU) content for the awareness and consideration stages respectively embed themselves more naturally in people's buying journeys.

This part will be key later on. These brands build mindshare and affinity with buyers *well* before they are ready to buy, which is where the long tail of opportunity exists, and where it's relatively less competitive.

Everyone's journey is different
An important thing to keep in mind is that our potential customers will not all go through the buyer's journey

in the same order. Some may begin at the decision stage, and realise that they need to more research, moving them back to the consideration stage. Similarly, some may start at the awareness stage and instantly feel like they're ready to make a purchase and jump straight to the decision stage. What's important is to have a buyer-friendly content pool that supports them at every stage they may pass through.

1b. What is Content Marketing

According to the Oxford Dictionary, Content marketing is "a type of marketing that involves the creation and sharing of online material (such as videos, blogs, and social media posts) that does not explicitly promote a brand but is intended to stimulate interest in its products or services."

It refers to the strategy, processes, and assets created to attract, engage, and convert buyers along their buyer's journey by adding value to them.

Content marketing comes in multiple flavours across video, audio, written, image, and perhaps VR/AR soon enough. It is the pursuit of creating content that buyers can engage with to better educate (and entertain - more on that later) themselves as they go about finding a path to solving their challenge or attaining their goal. Some would call it "selling the way people want to buy", as it is natural, and buyer-led. This means that based on the buyer's journey stage someone is at, as well as the channel they are on, they may come across a related video, article, or podcast that promises to share more helpful information towards helping them solve their challenge.

This next section covers popular written, video, audio, and image content formats that can be part of your arsenal.

I. WRITTEN

Written content is the genesis of content marketing. It comes in multiple forms, here are some of its popular formats:

a. Blogs

I like to picture blogging as the Don Corleone of content marketing, and a timeless one at that. Blogs and articles (i.e text) are still the primary way that content gets crawled and indexed on the internet, specifically on major search engines, which proves how relevant it is to those who are searching for additional content to better educate them on the challenge they are trying to solve for themselves or their business. Research featured on *Wired* magazine shows that great blog headlines can increase traffic by as much as 500%. Blogging as an art form takes many shapes, and some popular ones include:

How-to articles
As the label says, these are articles that provide structured, often step-by-step, process-driven solutions to problems that customers enter in search,

or stumble across on social media. According to Moz, How-to style articles ranked 3rd in a study for headline clarity preferences.

Listicles

Listicles ranked 1st in that same study. Listicles are articles written in the form of a numbered list. Numbers often make things easier to grasp, and this is why we tend to gravitate towards article headlines like "3 ways to ..." or "the top 10 alternatives to..." or "23 reasons why you must...". Due to their popularity, listicles are colloquially referred to as *Buzzfeed-style* articles too. "There have been plenty of studies, split tests, and discoveries that dig into the data," said Neil Patel, "Headlines with numbers are clear winners every time."

Long-form articles

Long-form articles are a cornerstone of every successful content strategy, and according to CoSchedule long-form content ranks higher and engages more readers. From an SEO perspective, Hubspot analyzed ~6,000 of their own articles and reported that 2000-word articles got more backlinks and shares on social media. Marketers who write these articles commonly position them as definitive resources or "ultimate guides" on a specific topic. These are so designed to build trust and convey thought leadership with buyers who are bombarded with tons of choices to get their information online and are in pursuit of one curated go-to source. If they read this one guide, they ought to get the gist of everything they are trying to accomplish. "They perform better and add immense value to your audience by going beyond just scratching the surface," says Neil Patel.

This makes long-form a popular type of written content. They can also be used to drive more context, for example, "the *beginner's* guide to...", or "the *CEO's* guide to..." or "the *2020* guide to...".

Long-form article titles can vary greatly depending on the context. They also often serve an important SEO function when they are used as pillar pages in a topic cluster. In this scenario, the pillar page, according to Hubspot, "answers questions about a particular topic, but leaves room for more detail in subsequent, related cluster content". Going in-depth on pillar pages and topic cluster strategies are beyond the scope of this book, but definitely worth a read.

A word paints a thousand... no wait.
All B2B written content, regardless of form, broadly serves the same goal which is to add value to buyers across the awareness, consideration, and decision stages. In addition to your own website, there are

multiple channels where blogs are typically posted and shared, including LinkedIn, Facebook, Twitter, Medium, and Quora.

The format is so powerful that you see clever marketers finding ways to link back to articles on alternative channels such as Instagram (in the form of a long-form caption, set of stories, or link in bio), Soundcloud (link back to a website), and even Spotify (an audio shout out during a podcast to check out an article on our website).

b. Ebooks and Guides

While seemingly identical to "long-form" articles above, ebooks and guides are a stand-alone genre of their own. They are often created by marketers to be positioned as "premium" content, often found gated behind a form or chatbot, and available for download or access via email sign up.

The appeal of ebooks and guides, at least when they first started, was to provide stand-alone content that answers a high-priority problem or a burning question that the buyer had, which she can now get access to by downloading said ebook and consuming it like she would a mini-book.

It is often used as a lever to generate leads by virtue of collecting the website visitor's email address to nurture the relationship further after the ebook has been delivered - commonly via email. Examples of ebooks and guides include:

An actual ebook
These read like mini-books, complete with tables of contents, custom graphics, and page numbers. They aim to provide a plethora of high-value, well designed and polished information to the buyer by presenting it in a coherent and considered fashion.

Ebooks are notorious among marketers for taking a lot of time to produce due to the level of research and detail that is required, which is why some marketers often decide to take an ebook and "release it to the public" by turning it into a long-form blog post (see pillar pages above). The rationale here is that if the ebook is not serving the company as a lead magnet, it may serve differently by generating traffic.

Because of its long-form nature, un-gating ebooks often contributes to lower bounce rates which, among other things like SEO and topic relevance, will improve organic ranking, driving overall attention to the business.

Workbooks
Workbooks are like practical ebooks. They engage the buyer by leading them to complete exercises, answer questions, and other related inputs from them that would ultimately help get them closer to their end goal.

Whitepapers
According to Coschedule whitepapers are "research-based reports (typically longer than a blog post but shorter than an ebook) are a staple content format for marketers."

Some of the best white papers include sought after statistics and insights that are important especially to B2B buyers. B2B buyers may cite such reports internally, or in business presentation they give.

II. VIDEO
Video content is the current darling of the marketing world, with 45% of marketers planning to add YouTube to their content strategy in 2019. According to Google, some 70% of YouTube viewers watch videos for "help with a problem" they're having in their hobby, studies, or job. According to Business Insider, video will represent 82% of all IP traffic in 2021. Some popular video content types include:

How-to Videos

These educational videos are the video cousin to the how-to articles we've discussed earlier. They address a key pain point that a buyer would have, and offers a structured solution to it.

Depending on the style of the video, they may be scripted or free-styled. They typically feature one person, but may also feature more than one, once again depending on the style and structure that the marketer has planned. How-to videos double as great content to include in articles as well, to provide a variety of media on the one page for the buyer to select how they would like to engage.

Interview-style Videos

Interview-style videos, as the name suggests, are videos where a host interviews 1 or more guests.

Interview-style videos can manifest their way in many forms, including interviews with customers, interviews with influencers, fireside chats, panel discussions, talk shows, and more.

One of the core benefits of interview-style videos is the built-in distribution that comes with having an additional person [or company] that will participate in the circulation of the video on social media after the fact. We will dive deeper into this topic later on.

<u>Vlogs</u>

These have been around for a while now, but are refreshingly original when it comes to brands. Vlogs can take on many forms, but they are essentially selfie-style videos that an individual would record to give personal opinions, thoughts, and an overall "behind the scenes" experience for their viewers.

Vlogs' original home is arguably YouTube, but nowadays we can find CEOs and other senior executives posting their vlogs on LinkedIn, Instagram, and their company websites. Vlogs help build affinity, trust, and loyalty with viewers over time, as they get used to seeing the same person (read: brand) over and over - assuming they are showing up with content that is appealing and value-adding in one way, shape or form.

III. AUDIO

Audio content (podcasts) are on a meteoric rise, we'll discuss leveraging this powerful format more in depth later in the book. In 2018 alone, according to FastCompany there were over 525,000 active shows and over 18.5 million episodes created. Audio podcasts are the modern-day radio shows, where both the marketers (and the buyers) get to choose what they will talk about and what they will consume - respectively.

Audio podcasts are great as they can be created once and syndicated across popular streaming platforms such as Soundcloud, Spotify, and iTunes. It instantly appeals to an often untapped audience that prefers to consume content during their daily routines, whether in their cars while commuting, in their headphones at the gym, or even at home via Google Home or Amazon Alexa devices.

The hands-free nature of audio content appeals to productivity-nerds. According to Podcast Insights, podcast listeners are loyal, affluent, and educated. Further, according to Podcast Insights, 80% listen to all or most of each podcast episode.

Barista playlists

A more offbeat way to create audio content is to curate [branded] music playlists that would be appealing to our buyer persona's interests, lifestyle and pace of life. For example, CoffeeCompany (a popular cafe chain in the Netherlands) has their amazing, barista-created playlists that you'd hear in their cafes also available on Spotify - so that you can relive the great experience you had at their cafe whenever you want. It's easy to say, imagine how a yoga studio may apply the same principle, but it doesn't stop there.

With enough creativity, we can come up with a "Frank Sinatra Fridays" playlist for a financial services firm, if that matches what their buyer persona would enjoy.

IV. IMAGE

Image content is also an O.G in the content world. Images are an excellent creative medium for marketers to leverage and figure out how best to make the most of - depending on their audience interests. 40.2% of marketers who were surveyed said that the visuals which performed best were actually original graphics, according to Venngage.

A thousand words

Not only do pictures speak a thousand words, but they instantly stand out in a sea of text whether placed in a blog post or shared on social media. So much in fact, that research shows the human brain processes visuals 60,000 times faster than text. Some popular image content types include:

Infographics

Infographics provide an easy medium for people to quickly consume a lot of information that is important to them. This could be anything from relevant industry statistics, new research, or even a visual summary of a process on how to accomplish something - think frameworks, roadmaps, and even step by step guides.

They're also "30 times" more likely to be viewed than a purely textual article according to Progressive Content.

Infographics can be posted on their own on social as commonly as they are found accompanying articles. Finally, infographics are highly shareable as they are visually appealing and provide a burst of value in one go.

Poster Quotes

Taking a memorable quote from an article, an interview, podcast, or other source and turning that into an image constitutes a poster quote. These can be illustrations or feature an image of the person being quoted. They are great and once again highly shareable especially if the person being quoted is an influencer or someone that is generally held in high regard by the target buyer persona. Moreover, poster quotes that feature quotes from notable people in your industry (or people that your persona would generally hold in high regard) leverages the often underestimated positive effects of social proof, which is one of the core tenets of influence as cited in Robert Cialidini's book of the same title.

1c. Why Marketers Shifted to Content

Content marketing was considered a significant shift for marketers - leading them in the direction of giving value first, and aligning to how buyers want to buy - when they want to buy. The concept of content itself however, was far from new.

"Content is not something that's been recently created," says Mark Kilens, VP of Content at Drift. "It's been around for decades. It goes back a 100+ years". Probably the most progressive transition was the "new" idea of creating content with the intent of building relationships, engagement, and trust - where not all content is designed for direct sales (or bottom of the funnel) purposes.

Credibility is built, not bestowed
A notable benefit of content creation is that it gives brands a creative opportunity to build credibility through social proof and associating with others that the buyer persona would care for. This includes, but is not limited to: people like them (customers?), influencers, and others in their domain. We'll unpack this more later on.

Counterintuitively, smart brands recognised that the more time is spent adding value with no hard-sells, the more buyers are prone to like, trust, and be influenced by the brand, as well as recommend to their friends who may seek their advice later down the line.

According to Wharton professor and word of mouth expert Jonah Berger, "Practical Value" is one of the main 6 drivers of word of mouth - when we come across something we believe will benefit a friend or colleague, we are more likely to share it with them as a recommendation because we want to be helpful. If you're interested in what makes certain ideas catch on like wildfire, I strongly recommend you pick up his bestseller book, *Contagious*. There, I just did it the practical value thing myself. Couldn't help it.

When done right, marketers can monitor key performance indicators from their content efforts to analyze traffic, lead, and customer conversion metrics using various marketing analytics tools

Content marketing helps serve multiple purposes for marketers, and we'll outline some of the most important ones below.

Brand Awareness

In today's world, your brand *is* the content you create. Specifically, the video, audio, written, and image content that is shared with people. Do you remember the days where all a brand needed was a website and the periodical ad on TV? That was a while ago. Today, more than two-thirds of marketing leaders say a strong brand is critical to their growth plans, according to LucidPress.

Brands today need to adopt a relentless *craftsman's mentality* to consistently create content that would add value to their buyers in the form of education, entertainment, or both. At the same time, every piece of content created (or lack thereof) is associated with our brand, which helps to drive attention, likability, trust, and if we're lucky, influence. Afterall, B2B companies that have strong perceived branding generate a higher EBIT margin than brands who are not, according to Forbes. Marketing Week found that B2B brands appeal more to customers when using emotional rather than rational messages in their marketing. 93% of brands continue to focus their content on marketing their own products and services, which doesn't help the B2B buyer research new ideas as cited by G2 in a published article.

According to the Content Marketing Institute, content is one of the most effective ways to promote a business, with 61% of US online consumers making a purchase after reading recommendations on a blog. 77% of internet users read blogs and content marketing is six times as effective in generating conversions than other methods. As Simon Sinek famously said, people don't buy what you do, they buy *why* you do it.

Applying that to brand awareness, businesses can use content as a creative and expressive medium to appeal to a specific buyer persona by demonstrating empathy and relatability to their challenges and goals that they are after.

When done right, the content would not only resonate deeply with their buyer but would attract many others like them; who think like them and have similar goals as well. Such is the power of building targeted brand awareness meant for a select tribe of people.

Thought Leadership
Content marketing is widely regarded as a vehicle to build thought leadership too. According to LinkedIn, "almost 60% of business decision makers said that thought leadership directly led to their awarding of business to an organization".

By strategically picking certain topics to create a volume of content around, marketers can build thought leadership in areas that play to a company's strengths, or even use it as a way to grow thought leadership in new domains, markets, and geographies. This has a positive impact on existing customers as well. LinkedIn also reported that more than half of business decision makers admitted to increasing their business based solely on their thought leadership in a domain.

Overall, it aims to provide buyers with content that they can come to trust over time as the go-to source on a topic. As brands understand, being top of mind more often than not tips the scale in their favour when it comes time to making a purchase decision.

In fact, according to Demand Gen Report, 96% of B2B buyers clearly stated they want content with more input from industry thought leaders. Thought leaders are trusted in their domains of expertise, and buyers are always actively seeking them. When they are exposed to them enough, they may often search for them by name (whether it's a company or a personal brand) to see what they have to say on a certain topic.

If I'm researching a topic around conversational marketing, I may do a general search, but I may likely go straight to Drift's website to see if my question was covered. If I'm looking for an expert opinion on a podcast mic I'm considering to buy, I may go to Podcastage - the YouTube creator - who reviews just about every known podcast microphone out there. You get the idea.

We all have our own go-to thought leaders on different topics without realizing it. It's more nuanced than we think. Sometimes we just look out for their content in our IG stories and LinkedIn feeds. We may not even think of them as "thought leaders", other than they are brands or individuals that we just really admire or like. Their content may subtly manifest itself in the form of social accounts we follow, blogs we're subscribed to by email, YouTube channels, and other online platforms.

<u>Lead Generation</u>

Free food: an obsession
When you walk into a supermarket, did you ever stop to get a nibble at one of those stands offering out free food samples on toothpicks? I'm talking Cheese cubes. Honey. Chutney. Cold cuts. Man, I was obsessed with those when I was a kid, and still am today. You may not agree with me, but I think all supermarket products should do that. After all, it's a great form of lead-gen.

In a B2B buyer's journey, after attention comes likability and trust. B2B marketers understand that lead-gen is a core step in being able to capture and qualify oncoming traffic to their website and social platforms. Landing pages are used strategically by 68% of B2B businesses to acquire leads according to Marketo.

This can be in the form of merely signing up to a brand's newsletter, or it could be getting access to a downloadable or premium asset that the brand has created such as an ebook, checklist, guide, tool, or even gated set of videos, podcasts, and articles. Content marketing is often regarded as the prime catalyst to get inbound, organic leads. Perhaps because it happens on the buyer's own time, when *they* are ready. Businesses today take steps to qualify leads, by virtue of getting them to answer more questions upfront commonly through a chatbot or online form.

The perceived value exchange has to be balanced enough for them to be motivated to share their information. Simply put, if the buyer thinks the gated content piece is worth the exchange, they will sign up and in turn become a lead for that business. With marketing automation, more sophisticated, buyer-led content journeys are now crafted to guide customers along the buyer's journey from awareness through to decision, based on their behaviour towards certain content.

Each guide, set of videos, or playbook is often attuned to the buyer's journey stage. Marketers commonly use such opt-ins as qualification signals to take someone from say, a lead, to a marketing qualified lead (MQL). Many B2B marketing/sales teams follow integrated structures such that MQLs are deemed "Sales-ready", which may get passed on to sales to be tracked as an opportunity in their pipeline. Other brands take a more data-driven approach, whereby leads are assigned an automated "score" based on the activities they take, which commonly includes how many [content] pages they view.

Often times, certain scores are given based on which content pieces are consumed, based on historical data that people who consume certain pages and topics are better-qualified leads. None of this is possible without content marketing, and it creates a great feedback loop for marketing and sales alike to track what converts best and do more of it.

Sales Enablement

Sales enablement is the content, technology and processes that help salespeople become more productive and successful. In some sales processes, outreach takes a more account-based approach, where the company would reach out first, rather than the prospect stumbling across the content via search or social media. In scenarios like that, and congruent with the popular Inbound Sales methodology (Identify, Connect, Explore, Advise), adding value at the beginning of the relationship sometimes starts with the salesperson recommending content pieces that were previously created by the company to address a pain point or curiosity that the buyer has.

As you may expect, many buyers are often receptive to this add-value-first style of communication, which increased the demand for content marketing; especially when it can now double as sales collateral. Based on the effectiveness of certain pieces, marketing teams can double down on certain topics and invest their resources accordingly to support overall brand awareness as well as sales efforts. It's so important in fact, that 58% of the deals in the average pipeline are derailed at some point because the sales department is not able to offer tailored content for each future customer - according to Sirius Decisions. On the bright side, sales and marketing alignment can help businesses become 67% better at closing deals according to Marketo.

So far we've looked at the change in the modern buyer's journey, a bird's eye view on content marketing and some of its various types, and why brands are and continue to gravitate to content in droves. But to really understand why it's never been a better time (and more important) for brands to build their own original series, we have to understand what led us to this, and to explore the necessity as well as the dark side of content marketing, in the next chapter.

"It is possible to have too much of a good thing."

– Aesop, Greek storyteller

2. Content Marketing: The Good and the Not So Good

2a. Content Has Never Been More Important

Today's world is filled with content like never before. Content from friends, family, celebrities, brands, and everyone in between is creating it. It's become a language of its own. No longer do people talk about the benefits of content, it is clear that this is the single best way to communicate and broadcast their experiences, ideas, and add value to others. Consider how much content is posted every 60 seconds according to Smart Insights:

- 500 hours of video uploaded to YouTube
- 3.3M Facebook posts
- 65.9K Instagram posts
- 448K Twitter posts
- 1.4K Blogs on Wordpress [alone]

Content creation as a way of life.
The reason why is because, whether individuals or brands, creating content has become a natural part of everyday life. Content is the defacto primary method to communicate new ideas, drive action, build

likability, trust, and develop memorable brands overall. People now judge brands by the content that they create (or lack thereof), specifically on a topic that they may be in the market to learn more about or get better familiarized with.

Have we gotten to a stage where brands have now over-realised the importance of creating content?

According to the State of Inbound 2018 report, 55% of marketers say blog content creation is their top inbound marketing priority. 61% of B2B marketers increased their use of social media in 2019, and a whopping 90% of B2B content marketers prioritize their audience's needs over their sales message when creating content.

Competing over content.
In a world of unlimited content, it's no longer enough to create "good" content, marketers are under unprecedented pressure to create "great" content in great quantities, on as many distribution channels as they can.

Wait, every social channel? Is that needed?

As any good consultant would tell you, it depends. Though, more often than not the answer is a resounding yes - brands need to create content for all major social channels.

"Our customers aren't on Spotify"
In B2B, people often hear their boss, colleagues, or even friends in the industry say "our customers aren't on Instagram". Or a similar one, "our customers are serious, they're only on LinkedIn and are not on Facebook". Or, "our customers aren't on Spotify".

To navigate this, clever B2B marketers are recognizing that buyers are humans too; that they are not their day jobs.
Although obvious, it is often overlooked. They have lives outside their jobs where they enjoy other pastimes. They may listen to Spotify, spend hours on Instagram, and watch videos of Labradoodles tucking babies to sleep in their Facebook feeds like the rest of us.

Picture a CEO of an accountancy firm on her weekend, and she's accompanying her partner as he picks out a few new shirts. While she waits outside the changing room, she finds herself checking Instagram, and comes across an image post that reads "the 10 most innovative accountancy firms that are killing it right now, link in bio". Next thing we know, she could be navigating to that brand's profile, and yes, clicking the link in bio to see what can be learnt from this article. Perhaps she's curious how she can get her own firm featured as well. You get the idea.

A chef may do something similar, watching YouTube videos on other styles of cooking he was always curious about on the train home.

A real estate broker may start tuning into the same real-estate Spotify podcast his buddy told him about over WhatsApp because he figured it's a productive way to spend his morning commutes into work.

This happens all the time. Yet many people still think that doctors only read "doctor magazines", or that HR managers only read HR blogs and only tune their attention to HR online groups and forums.

While such outlets may naturally get their attention, brands will always have a tactical advantage over other players in the industry by merely recognising that buyers are humans too. This instantly expands the possibilities at our disposal when it comes to content.

There are unlimited ways that our buyer persona can consume content across all popular online channels. These popular channels are the ones you and I are thinking of right now, which include the likes of

Google Search, Facebook, LinkedIn, Instagram, YouTube, Quora, Medium, Twitter, Pinterest, Soundcloud, Spotify, and iTunes. Our buyer persona is very likely on most if not all of those. Smart brands don't take any chances on their revenue goals for the year and create content for all the above.

So how come buyers are always switched on, even on the less obvious channels in their off-work hours? Here are two possible explanations.

Explanation 1. Maslow's hierarchy of needs
Simply put, and as Maslow's hierarchy of needs taught us people have a natural instinct towards self-actualisation and becoming the best version of themselves in various aspects of life. Of course, before self-actualization comes other types such as esteem-based needs (e.g: getting a promotion), belonging and social needs (e.g: keeping up with peers), and safety/basic needs (e.g: keeping my job).

People want to do the best job they can, and to hit the next goal or overcome the next challenge, they formulate questions and then find (or stumble across) content that gets them closer to the solution.

Naturally, the content producers often are the ones who sell products or services that provide those solutions. Common B2B expressions of that are, getting a promotion, getting better team alignment, proving the contribution of the department to the overall organization, or just growth of their business. On the other hand, if I don't do well I may be fired, or generally face a risk - and so on.

Explanation 2. Craftsmanship
Some people genuinely love what they do (gasp!) and they're always looking to learn more, aiming for increasingly ambitious goals on personal, company, or industry level. They're like craftsmen, obsessed with creating great work, and are endlessly loyal to it as they identify deeply with the fruit of their labour.

Some have a passion to do things differently, to be outliers in their industry, and to stand out and build a legacy as such. Others simply enjoy the rhythm of making sure they're always sharp in their industry and understand the latest trends, with the agility to resolve challenges as they arise. They understand that to do so they need to familiarise themselves with their goals and challenges by consuming relevant content on the topics they're passionate about.

With this over-realisation of the importance of content, comes an immediate sense to create content everywhere the target audience may spend their attention.

Because of the omnichannel content that exists, in a way, it's never been more important to create content, if at least to stand out from other content that is already out there.

Sounds fatiguing right? That doesn't make it untrue.

2b. Content Marketing is Getting Harder

The real ROI (and cost) of content marketing

Back when I was in college studying marketing, I remember my uncle would call me from Egypt to check on me, as well as to deliver the piss-take of the day:

"Hey, how's the advertising going? Can you get me some of those free promo mugs you're giving away?"

If it wasn't mugs, it was branded backpacks, and anything else he envisioned me to spend all day doing.

He's not entirely wrong, I guess. There was a time when "giving away free promotional stuff" represented a large part of a marketer's job description.

Today though, marketing's role and specifically content marketing has never been more important for small brands and corporates alike. Long gone are the days where brands did not understand the value of marketing or were able to measure the ROI.

A different time

There was a time when marketing was not fully understood, and at best was regarded as a luxury afforded by bigger brands. brands now are recognizing how content marketing is a key step in enabling sales and building scalable brand recognition, trust, and lead pipeline. brands now leverage various social and content tools that help create, publish, track, and analyze content against any objectives and key results (OKRs) that are core to their success. We discussed in the last chapter how important and widespread content marketing has become.

Now the plot twist...

Somewhere along the way, it has become so easy to start creating content, that it's become difficult again.

<>

Really difficult, infact.

Because the barriers to entry are so low, anyone and everyone can and is doing content. With the unlimited amount of content supply, the bar was raised higher for what is deemed "quality" content.

This means marketers have to now spend more time and resources in ensuring their content stands out and delivers, leading to an endless vicious cycle led by the highest bidder (or perhaps the best-organized team). Ironically, this means that once again marketers have to prove the value of their content marketing efforts.

Think of it as a top athlete playing college basketball star having to prove himself all over again now that he's made it to the NBA. To overcome this, we need to familiarise ourselves with the three external factors at play:

- Competitors
- Customers
- Resources

1. Competitors

There's a reason why venture capital firms care a great deal about whether an early-stage startup they're considering to add to their portfolio has competitors or not. Competition in healthy doses can be a good thing for a number of reasons, including validating a market's size and potential.

Competitors compete for mind share during the buyer's journey by creating as much quality content as they can. Once brands started seeing results from the inbound way of thinking and content marketing, it only made it more difficult for existing players to maintain their stature as well for new entrants to get discovered by the people who most need what they buy amidst the noise, purely based on the unlimited supply of content now available to buyers.

On a marketing department level, it made it much harder to show results and therefore ROI from investment in marketing, due to the volume of me-too content. Hubspot suggests around 6 months of consistent, relentless content production and optimization in order to start seeing results from inbound. It may take brands even longer depending on the competitive landscape. This is where going niche, blue ocean, and doubling down on brand pays off. Nevertheless, competition makes it more difficult to show the ROI of content marketing. Joe Pulizzi advises, "without "tilting" your content just enough to truly have a different story to tell, your content will fade into the rest of the clutter and be forgotten."

2. Customers

Potential customers are experts, albeit subjective, at assessing whether the content they consume is quality to them or not. Realistically no one watches a video or reads an infographic saying "ah, this is quality!" rather - validation of quality manifests itself more subtly, such as deciding to navigate to the homepage of that brand to learn more after watching a related YouTube video, or reading more than one blog posted on the brand's website, and so on.

Marketers may monitor that in the form of traffic visits, bounce rate, conversion rate, and so on. The customer is always right. They get their vast experience from the volume of content they consumed relating to their interests, goals, and challenges.

When another brand comes along with content, they would have seen a fair share of articles, videos, or podcasts to be able to make a call on whether this "new" piece of content is worth their attention and trust, and more fundamentally, whether it adds anything new to them.

Because they have high standards, and because there is an unlimited supply of content, this drives the cost way up to stand out (read: the true cost of content marketing), and on the other side of the coin - causes the ROI of such an investment to trend down.

3. Resources

This one is straightforward. Let's be conservative and consider this a purely external factor based on budget, headcount, and other circumstances within the company. Marketers have to constantly find creative ways to stay top of mind, gain mindshare and build thought leadership.

All this leads to generating tangible results for their team and the company within the allocated budget, and with the accessible talent they have in-house. Because brands need money to make money (and content), project managing resources efficiently to create the highest quantity and quality of content is always tough for brands when other competitors may be better funded or better organized, thus making the ROI and cost of content marketing an uphill battle, and a bit of a catch-22. 27% of marketers say securing enough budget is their top marketing challenge according to Hubspot.

Ignoring content marketing is sadly not an option
It's not as simple as moving to the next shiny thing, content marketing is here to stay.

According to Social Media Today and Marketing Week, 91% of total ad spend is viewed for less than a second. As a result of that, $38 billion in digital ad spend was "wasted" in 2017. Wistia CEO Chris Savage mentioned at the start, "Digital advertising today is an arms race with diminishing returns". While paid ads can be effective when done right, all roads ultimately lead back to content marketing as the bedrock of building long-lasting brand and results, as opposed to renting attention on a pay-per-action basis.

Remember the 7/11/4 rule

Hubspot reported that 47% of buyers look at 3-5 pieces of content before buying. Daniel Priestley calls it the 7/11/4 rule - citing research from Google's Zero Moment of Truth - that buyers need to experience a brand for 7 hours, 11 touchpoints, and ideally in 4 different creative mediums (video, blog, audio, written) before they start to fully trust a brand or become a client.

Furthermore, 65% of senior executives navigate to a site after viewing a related Youtube video, according to Single Grain. If that's not enough, content marketing is proven to get at least three times more leads than paid search advertising according to the Content Marketing Institute. Especially when a product or industry is part of a longer (3+ months) or complex sales cycle, people prefer to do their own research and arrive at their own conclusions before going ahead with a purchase, or re-purchase.

A note on existing and repeat customers

Content continues to be of paramount importance post-sales as well. As B2B SaaS product marketers would agree, it may mean the difference between a customer churning to join a competitor or deciding to continue with their current subscription. Post-sales content includes onboarding, on-going product education, and use-cases.

Taming the content beast

My grandmother rest her soul used to lovingly say "Don't eat meat on its own, eat it with bread so you get full faster". It was one of our favourite phrases to repeat growing up as it provided a very practical solution whenever there wasn't enough meat to make us full, eat more carbs with it!

Because as the saying goes, if it's not broken don't fix it. If it's broken, we can usually tell. We'll see people try in various ways, although often suboptimal, to address their pain point. In this case, content marketing management comes with a few skeletons in its cupboard.

In a North American study carried out by the Content Marketing Institute, B2B marketers were asked about the factors contributing to decreased success over the year prior, 43% cited management/HR (including staffing issues), 47% cited content-creation challenges, and a whopping 57% cited not enough time devoted to content marketing as the top challenge. I only came across this study recently.

Prior to seeing this study, coincidentally, I did my own qualitative study, speaking with various brands across Europe and the US to understand how brands are going about solving their content marketing challenges - specifically the quantity and the quality components.

Namely, how are businesses keeping up with the need to create volumes of both high quality and quantity content pieces. The findings were congruent with what is already widely practised by organizations trying to correct this challenge, presented below:

1. Headcount

Expensive in the short-term

The Cloud 100 is an annual report by Forbes that rates the world's best private cloud brands based on a set of key metrics, including estimated valuation and market leadership. Drift analyzed that marketers represent

4.7% of a Cloud 100 company's workforce, as opposed to salespeople which represented more than double that percentage.

Continuing to grow an in-house marketing team can in many cases be the best long-term solution. In the short term, however, it can get pretty expensive pretty fast for brands.

Businesses that want to solve the content problem by growing their marketing headcount recognise that there are too many hidden costs associated for it to have an immediate pay-off. These include compensation and benefits costs, training costs, downtime and learning curve, along with other associated overheads. Naturally, this growth is most expensive especially for SMBs - that may not have a large dedicated marketing headcount budget ready to go at any given time.

For many fast growth-companies, we often see priority going to sales headcount, as they are seen as the primary revenue generators. Secondly, because of the external forces discussed earlier, marketing ROI is getting easier to "measure" using technology but harder to grow per se. Research from TrackMaven reports that over 70% of marketers cite attributing social and content to revenue as their top challenge.

It is often not a question of competence but rather a question of capacity. This, in turn, relates to how content is both a quantity and quality game - given the increased level of competition, a vicious never-ending cycle. If you think this is a sign of a broken system, I agree. It threatens some marketing teams to be seen as cost centers, and not the revenue-generators they likely are. As a result, this makes it harder to justify prioritizing new headcount for marketing.

Besides, assuming we are in a position to hire for marketing, how do we know that will magically solve our content challenge?

As marketers and creative teams tend to have siloed specialities (SEO, automation, paid, content writing, video production, graphic design) leadership are now asking themselves how much compounded content value will 1 or 2 more hires produce. What are the costs of that, and what are the true costs of that?

According to MarketingWeek, "Maximising success in any line of business today – not to mention providing the best possible experience to customers – requires that marketers and their colleagues make concerted efforts to break down silos and collaborate across functions."

Furthermore, it may cost significantly more per hire to find multifaceted or senior content professionals that have more than one focus or speciality of experience. For example, marketers who are both excellent writers as well as video editors. Perhaps there are alternative ways to approach this.

This excerpt from Michael Mankins of Bain & Company (as featured in Harvard Business Review) summarizes it perfectly:

"Instead of focusing on continuously managing the denominator, by cutting headcount, executives should identify ways to boost the numerator, and increase output. By systematically removing obstacles to productivity, deploying talent strategically, and inspiring a larger percentage of their workforce, leaders can dramatically improve productivity and reignite top-line growth."

Headcount isn't the problem, its whether all of the team's vectors are aligned and pushing towards the same direction, or if they're left fragmented - working in silos.

In another Harvard Business Review article, best-selling business strategy author Chris Zook advised that "if you take the time to codify your key practices and principles, and use them as a compass to help chart your course, you can help your company maintain a strong sense of purpose and a powerful consistency of action as you contend with overload."

In a related Forbes article, Joanne Markow, Partner at GreenMason shared that "If you're hiring ahead of the work and the work doesn't come through, that's a problem. Your eye on operations and its relationship to new business is absolutely key to growing in a smart way."

A write up by Inc on the dangers of growing too fast states that "[as] your ranks grow and positions that were filled by individuals transform into teams of people, the need to stay organized becomes amplified."

Amplifying inefficiencies

The question becomes, how can we value our existing team's time, strengths and expertise better? How can we build new processes that help compound their results, in a world where results from content are trending down not up? It's not us people that are the problem, it's what we ask our people to do; it's how best we make them shine as individuals and as a team - through their results.

How can we amplify their results?

If we keep hiring without improving our processes, we're <u>amplifying the inefficiencies</u> that existed in the first place. This means we amplify the cost and time needed to course-correct.

2. Agencies

Expensive in the long-term

Working with marketing agencies could be a plausible approach for many businesses regardless of their profile, but it too comes with hidden true costs.

It costs time and money to put together RFPs (Requests for proposals), arrange pitch sessions, review references, and finally select an agency within the budget allocated. After selection, it would be up to each business to train, coach, and approve work consistently. These 6, 12 or 24-month contracts don't (and perhaps aren't intended) to last forever.

Agencies could be great to work with but you need to be aware of what hidden true costs are involved and whether they make sense for your business based on the stage you're at.

One ongoing trend we're seeing is brands taking their content back in-house.

A 2018 global study conducted by Adobe and Econsultancy involving over 4000 marketing professionals reported that more advertisers plan on bringing content production in-house.

For many businesses, working with agencies is a short-term play until they bring someone in-house, or adopt processes that they can carry on by themselves.

A marketing agency could be a solid way for a business to find their feet and put some foundations of brand identity and online presence, but many brands know that deep down, this may not be the most cost effective long-term solution. Various per hour fees, retainers, while often designed to be ROI-centric, always keeps businesses measuring whether this is the best long-term solution to their pain point, in light of how many years they intend to be in business.

An article in Bizfluent summarizes some of the areas to be mindful of when working with agencies, including:

- True vs surface-level familiarity with your offering
- Clear vs ambiguous expectations
- Prioritizing you over other higher-paying clients
- One-size-fits-all creative thinking

Especially in the mid to long term, brands can't help but ask, "Could this be cheaper to bring in-house?" However, once they do, they may be met with the headcount challenges discussed earlier.

3. Do Nothing

Expensive in the short and long term

It would be easy to render ourselves helpless when it comes to content, except that's not an option, as we discussed earlier.

In choosing not to do anything, we lose in the short and long term with the people who most wanted to hear from us and do business with us. I found it tough to find many brands who said they are *not* planning to do any content marketing.

Word of mouth: A love/hate relationship
For most brands that believe reactive customer word of mouth alone would be sufficient in attracting new

business, they will not have the means to grow predictably. Rather, they will always resort to playing it by ear which in business can be synonymous with business suicide.

Bigger (or smarter) competition doing high volumes of quality content will generate more word of mouth, and progressively limit your market share, reducing addressable opportunity and resulting in lost potential revenue.

Word of mouth continues to be king, and brands that aren't doing content marketing are blocking themselves the opportunity to create scalable word of mouth assets in various rich media formats.

According to a large North American study carried out on B2B content marketing, when asked whether organizations expect to create more or less content, only 2% expected to create less content. 25% said they intend on producing the same amount, and a majority of 70% stated they will be creating more content.

Growing headcount or working with agencies are both solutions that have their pros and cons, like anything in life. Fundamentally it comes down to the overarching strategy that makes your processes effective in the first place.

Before we dive into the topic of original series, we need to first talk about one of the main reasons, though little discussed, that compels us as marketers to think differently about content in the first place.

That reason is burnout.

2c. Why Marketers Often Experience Burnout

According to Mayoclinic:

"Job burnout is a special type of work-related stress — a state of physical or emotional exhaustion that also involves a sense of reduced accomplishment and loss of personal identity."

Given the external factors we've explored thus far of increased competition, heightened customer sensitivity to content, and internal resources limitations, the feeling of reduced accomplishment often rings loud and true for marketers.

It is hard to stand out making content the old way
It's true. In a noisy world where everyone is producing content around their products and services—it is getting harder and harder to get people to give us their attention.

Also. We owe goldfish an apology.

Goldfish can retain information for 9 seconds. We don't have the memory of a goldfish. According to a study by Microsoft, research shows that the average human attention span has fallen from 12 seconds (in 2000) to only 8 seconds..

We have never had more me-too blogs and content than today:

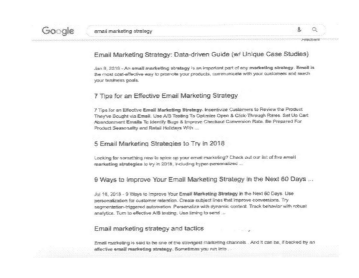

In 2017, Search Engine Journal published an article stating, "Organizations are demanding ever-higher performance from their digital marketing teams. People are trying to comply, but the usual method – putting in longer hours – has backfired". A huge burden on marketing teams today is to consistently create content. But why does creating content, something that was originally meant to be creative, thought-leading, and expressive, end up being so awfully draining for us?

For-profit brands are commonly structured around increasing growth and profitability YoY, which on a field level is often reflected in the form of increased targets and increased expectations. Achieving success is not a static goal, but rather a dynamic set of KPIs that increase periodically. The goal post keeps moving for industries, which naturally has a ripple effect on internal teams as well. This definitely contributes to the stress felt by marketers.

The "content success" trio

When it comes to content success (and therefore the stress of pursuing it) it's down to balancing three elements: quality, frequency, and distribution. When all three work in lockstep, fireworks happen. trio presents us with the core of any successful content strategy that we have to keep in lockstep.

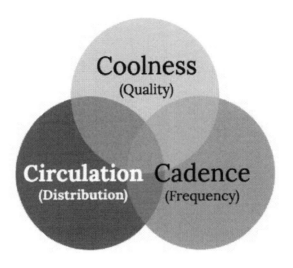

1. Coolness (or Quality)

The first challenge we face is the need to constantly come up with content that is deemed relevant and engaging by our target audience. We need to think outside of the box like our results depend on it.

Cool or die

The articles, videos, or images we publish have to be unwaveringly crafted for our buyer persona, and be deemed valuable by them. Otherwise, in a sea of sameness in content, it'll be an uphill battle to stand out.

Especially in competitive spaces, marketers need to spend time studying all the content that is currently published on a certain topic, often by their direct competitors, and then dedicate considerable time and effort to identifying gaps that could be worth leveraging to create their new content piece.

Some of the research methods that marketers use in the pursuit of upping their content's authority and quality include:

- Conducting keyword research - to identify high volume, low difficulty keywords and topics to craft content around, primarily targeted towards search engines.
- Doing outreach for backlinks - often seen as a necessary evil, marketers often dedicate endless hours to manually build links back to existing content that they created to boost the URL and website strength.
- Going more niche - finding ways to go deeper on a topic and appeal to more long-tail queries in pursuit of context.
- Studying competitor blogs and social profiles - to get inspiration, emulate, or identify gaps in their content that can be worth leveraging.

All the above methods work, and some are even essential, but are we really at an advantage when all of our competitors are putting in similar effort towards doing the same thing? This too is a leading contributor to the exhaustion marketers feel.

The best content created by brands is the selfless kind. The kind that focuses purely on the buyer persona and their interests. As Dale Carnegie once said, "You can make more friends in two months by becoming interested in other people than you can in two years by trying to get other people interested in you."

Stop interrupting, start entertaining

"Quality" content should mean something new for all of us. We should seek to maintain a balance of entertainment and utility. While there are some pieces of content that can be purely educational, according to SEMrush, if your target audience is millennials (born between 1977 and 2000) then creating entertaining content needs to be a core part of your strategy.

Entertaining content, as we will soon see, doesn't need to be humorous per se. But it *does* need to be gripping and highly contextual to the conversations and self-talk our buyer personas are having towards attaining their goals.

Static Goals vs Self Actualization

Are we guilty of oversimplifying what our buyer persons are after? Do we simply look at the "static" goals they're after?

What if we recognize that our buyer personas have much more sophisticated, nuanced interests, beyond attaining specific goals - that equally influence how much they like and relate to a brand? If we're capable of doing that, we enable ourselves to begin thinking deeper about their psychographics, and what the pursuit of self-actualization looks like for our buyer personas. In that we can uncover lots of great opportunities to create quality content that are not as obvious, helping you get a leg up on the competition. If you ever noticed some of your favourite brands talking about things that they don't even sell products or services for, then you've experienced that. You will see how episodic content is a great vehicle to put this into practice and cement your brand in the minds of customers.

2. Cadence (or Frequency)

The content hamster wheel

I've certainly been there as a marketer. Probably the biggest source of "content stress" for businesses creating content is the frequency piece. No issue creating one or even a few blogs and videos. It's the constant grind of having to put out post after post to save the momentum from dying.

Sharon Hurley Hall cited in an article for OptinMonster that 32% of marketers think their content creation workflow is fair or poor (according to Content Marketing Institute), and that two thirds of people find it hard to produce content on a consistent basis (according to Zazzle Media).

Let's take a sharp left here, and address a related question that may have popped into your mind at one point:

How much content should we be putting out anyway?

GaryVee advocates, "If you are not producing 100 pieces of content … every single day you are leaving the greatest opportunity in the world on the table," and I couldn't agree more.

According to Convince&Convert, a smart way to think about it is to come up with a list of FAQ questions that your buyer persona may have, well into the 100s, and use that as a starting point.

This makes sense since the more content you can create the more top of mind your brand will be. This is especially compounded in importance in competitive markets where others are already putting out content.

On the flip side, this translates into added work and effort yet again for marketers, to be able to create content that is both shipped regularly but also maintains a certain standard of value of entertainment and/or utility.

Some of the methods that marketers use in the pursuit of upping their content's frequency include:

- Setting monthly and quarterly content targets
- Planning quarterly or yearly social calendars
- Creating content offers + promoting them
- Creating events + promoting them
- Repurposing existing content (more on this later)

3. Circulation (or Distribution)
The 3rd element of the content success trio is, of course, making sure that the right people see your content. This involves thinking about leveraging owned, earned, and paid media to get in front of those people.

Owned Media
These are the distribution channels that are your "own". It includes things like:

- Your company's website
- Your company's social media accounts
- Your employees' social media accounts

Earned Media

Great content gets picked up and circulated by others. This is the holy grail of marketing distribution and is referred to as earned media. It includes things like:

- Social media shares
- Social media mentions
- News features/ PR
- Mentions in other blogs/media outlets
- Reviews

Paid Media

Paid Media is what it says on the label. It includes things like:

- PPC (Pay Per Click) Ads
- Display Ads
- Remarketing Ads
- Social Media Advertising
- Paid Influencers
- Sponsored Content

After spending a lot of time and effort in creating quality content that is maintained at a high frequency, the last thing we want is for our target audience to not see it.

In the case of owned media, it is important to ensure our content is visible on all of the social media networks that we are active on so that our audience can see it. The more social media outlets we can craft content around, the more shelf life our content will have and the more people will see it.

When it comes to earned media, brands often need to build relationships with other blogs, influencers, and even their own brand advocates to share the content created to amplify its reach and distribution. This takes a lot of time, especially when we have a lot of content to promote. It can also be hit or miss because we never know what will work and what won't until we launch it, which contributes to the feeling of burnout at times.

Most brands often have an ability over just one or two of the three. To nail all three every month is a struggle without a proven process designed to tackle them.

To balance all at once can be tricky when adopting a traditional content marketing approach of static content calendars, or worse, ad-hoc creating and posting.

As promised, there is a light at the end of the tunnel (funnel?), and we're just about ready to go there now.

"The real voyage of discovery consists not in seeking new lands but in seeing with new eyes."

– Marcel Proust, French novelist

3. Stop Creating Content. Start Creating Shows

3a. A Simple Mindset Shift

At this stage in the book, we find ourselves in a pickle.

On the one hand, we know that content is the most effective and sustainable way to grow a business and show ROI from marketing. On the other hand, we know that it's never been more difficult to create content, due to various external and internal factors. Yet, we equally know that *not* creating content is not an option.

The year was 347 BC, and the place was Athens. Aristotle was developing the legendary body of work which would later become known as The *Rhetoric*. It is an ancient Greek enquiry on the art of persuasion. You may have heard of it. It's where ethos, pathos, and logos come from, which are Aristotle-coined terms.

Ethos - Those elements grounded in credibility and trust.

Pathos - Those elements grounded in emotions, and psychology.
Logos - Those elements grounded in logic, data and statistics

Fast forward to 2001. Carmine Gallo's book *Talk Like Ted*, revealed an exciting finding. In the book, a survey of all the best TED talks (and speakers) found that they had one critical element in common: 65% of their talks focused on *pathos* - storytelling. *Logos* represented 25%, while *ethos* represented only 10%.

In 2016, a fascinating study from MIT Review revealed that all films, books, and TV series, in essence, follow only one of 6 story plots. Yet, you and I probably have our favourite films and books and regard them as 'originals'. Even if the data shows that they are 6 story plots, it's how they were *packaged* that makes them exciting and fresh. Same goes for Netflix and HBO series.

What if we apply that thinking to how we create content? Forget everything they taught us about content and marketing. What if your business can have its own show or original series? Afterall, we're not just competing for attention from our competitors. As far as our buyer is concerned, we're competing for attention with everything in their world; we're competing for attention with Netflix.

White flag, right? Not quite.

You see, some brands made a different observation. They thought,

"Netflix has original series. What if we start creating our own original series too?"

Content that is inherently grounded in storytelling, entertainment, and memorable, loveable characters.

Think like a producer not a marketer

What if we start thinking not in terms of blogs, images, and videos, but in terms of episodes? How will marketing improve? How will sales improve? And how fast would we be able to grow thought leadership?

In a sea of sameness and content pieces created in silos, people will gravitate towards your original series. It would be easier to consume, more organized, richer, and put simply, more fun. "Shows are built with the express goal of holding attention," says Jay Acunzo, founder at Marketing Showrunners, "which in turn earns trust, which in turn triggers action, which helps the business."

In the next sections, we will explore what episodic content is, it's hidden benefits, and what it means for your business. Finally, we'll explore how to begin building your own original series, measuring your results, and selling this internally.

3b. What is Episodic Content

In the early months of 1933, only a few days after his inauguration, U.S President Franklin D. Roosevelt was faced with a major challenge. Bank closings were hurting families nationwide, which all started due to people losing their confidence in banks and withdrawing their money in droves, all at the same time. Congress passed the Emergency Banking Act and Roosevelt introduced something called federal deposit insurance in an effort to restore stability to the banking system. He knew that he still had to win back the public's confidence in banks.

He decided to address them directly over the radio, in what would become the first instalment of a series of 30 evening radio addresses which have been come to known as FDR's *Fireside Chats.*

On the same evening when the Emergency Banking Act was passed, President Roosevelt reached an estimated 60 million in his first chat to explain to them what took place, and how a resolution has been reached, to re-instil their trust in the banking system - to return their money to the bank.

As a result of his first fireside chat, historian William L. Silber writes, what took place next was "[a] remarkable turnaround in the public's confidence ... The contemporary press confirms that the public recognized the implicit guarantee and, as a result, believed that the reopened banks would be safe, as the President explained in his first Fireside Chat." President Roosevelt succeeded in changing the minds of millions of people, safely restoring more than half of the cash that people were personally holding on to.

His original series was a hit.

The name *Fireside Chats* was first coined by people in the press and later used by the public, and eventually the President himself. Roosevelt's press secretary first inspired the term, when he expressed that these chats made the audience feel like they were sitting right there by the fireside as the President drew them close, entrusting them with his thoughts on national affairs.

One of the huge appeals of Roosevelt's Fireside Chats was how down-to-earth they were, speaking to people in terms of their day-to-day interests, to build rapport and relatability. President Roosevelt would go on to make 29 more iconic episodes in the form of evening radio addresses. It was used to build a direct link of confidence, trust, and influence with his audience - the people of the United States.

President Franklin D. Roosevelt Fireside Chats was one of the earliest forms of purpose-built episodic content, designed to inspire, engage, influence, and drive action.

Today, **Episodic Content** (or "branded series") can be defined as creating sequential, engaging video or audio content that is part of a series centred around a certain theme or topic—similar to a series you'd find on platforms such as Netflix, YouTube, or Spotify.

In business, episodic content can help brands accelerate visibility, shorten sales cycles, and stay resource-effective all in lockstep. Instead of worrying about what to blog about next, or what to post on social today, smart CEOs and CMOs are building episodic content and putting on film-director hats, because they know not many people are thinking that way - yet.

Their content strategy became their show strategy, and vice versa.

A big blue ocean
Right from the offset, this blue ocean way of thinking can help brands stand out from others in their industry

who are still creating ad-hoc content with no clear structure or style. The brands that create episodic content shows strategically remove themselves from the content rat race with competitors and create "original series" around their buyer personas' core interests instead.

By mentally changing our focus from content strategy to "original series", we too can start to see things differently.

I like to think of it as, "let's stop creating content - and start creating shows". It fundamentally changes the way we marketers have been approaching content creation for the last two decades. Even though episodic content itself is not new.

Episodes could be anywhere from 5 mins to 30 mins - even longer, based on the type of show being put together.

The best episodic content is entertaining as much as it is educational. In a time where many brands rush to educate before building trust and likability, creating content that is designed to be entertaining helps accustom viewers to the brand by naturally capturing their attention and interest before anything else. By entertaining their personas first, they build attention, likability, and trust—helping them gain permission to give more education throughout the customers' buying journey where it really matters.

Episodic content is the ultimate storytelling vehicle to helps you be more creative, and therefore more effective, in your marketing strategy and in attracting the people that most need your business. There is one thing that all successful episodic series tend to have in common; a secret handshake of sorts.

The secret handshake
Brands that "get it" create episodic content that is not about their products and services, far from it. They don't even create content that directly answers their buyer persona's questions. It's too predictable. Besides, they know that such content has already been done. In order to build relatability and likability with their community, they go a level deeper. They create content that is focused on the *culture* surrounding their buyer persona and the industry they're in.

This gives them a canvas that's more open and creative. It's the small talk of content marketing: nuanced conversations that are engaging as much as they are insightful and just plain interesting. When done right, they make it easy for their persona to consume and share that content on, because it expresses the kind of people they are; what they're in to.

The 6-star podcast

A great example of that is Drift's original series Seeking Wisdom - hosted by David Cancel (CEO) and Dave Gerhardt (VP of Marketing). In their own words, its "A podcast from Drift all about personal and professional growth. From behind the scenes stories to book reviews to marketing, growth, and sales advice, Seeking Wisdom delivers 6 stars only." It's a great example of a brand that focuses on creating content that surrounds the *culture* that their customers are part of, rather than focusing blandly on products & services. Remember Carnegie's advice, that the more interested you are in people the faster they will be interested in you.

If I were me, which I am, what would I do?

There's an awesome factor at play when you make the decision to start your own original series. We love consuming things that say something about the kind of person we are. As Seth Godin says, we tell ourselves stories about what we do all the time. That is, we have an explanation for why we do certain things. Maybe it's a tribal thing. In his book *This is Marketing*, Godin reminds us that people often take action because they believe that 'people like us do things like this'.

This is hardly new.

This has its roots in classic marketing literature as far back as 1959 in S.J Levy's work *Symbols for Sale* - whereby customers often reinforce their identities through their consumption choices. It is often referred to as *symbolic consumption*: I am what I consume.

The most effective episodic content speaks *for* consumers in a favourable way. It may address burning questions they have, poke fun at pet peeves, address current events or external factors, and genuinely speak to the culture surrounding their dreams, fears, and curiosities.

'Solving for culture' is the goal of episodic content. As mentioned, it's not the kind of content that rushes to provide a solution. It is the kind of content though that takes the time to say "I feel you, bro, it's tough out there." or the kind that says "Girl, don't even get me started". It's empathetic at the core. That's where it gets its appeal and potential for word of mouth.

Gary Vaynerchuk is an episodic content pioneer. He frequently advocates that businesses should see themselves as media companies first and foremost. It's a sustainable way to have a never-ending well of content whether it includes just you, your guests, or both.

The types of shows you create can range from talk-show style series to documentary-style videos, and everything in between, which we will discuss in more detail shortly.

Depending on the style of show you have, you will find that the topics for the different episodes flow much easier. Allow me to explain.

If you design an original series podcast for your brand, each episode can be filmed with 1 or more guests. Examples of who your guests could be include influencers in your industry, target accounts, past customers, or anyone else that your buyer persona would be interested in or able to relate to. On the other hand, if you create a talking-head style series or vlog, you can draw inspiration from past blog posts around a pillar topic you wrote to turn those into episodes. You may also decide to create a reaction video series, where you react to current events pertaining to your customers' interests and curiosities.

When I asked Jay Acunzo why he believes businesses slowly gravitating towards building their own original series, he summed it up as follows:

"In sum, it's never been harder to grab attention, so we must focus on keeping those who do happen our way. When that's the goal, we need to create content and measure accordingly. Shows are the world's most proven vehicle for doing this.

In the end, brands reap two core benefits: The lifetime value of everyone they reach goes up, because those people stick, stay, and spend more time with the brand, and our customer acquisition costs go down thanks to word-of-mouth referrals provided by that loyal, passion audience. Just think about that: LTV goes up. CAC goes down. If you listen carefully, you can hear every CMO alive nodding furiously."

The beauty of episodic content is that it transcends industries, functions, company sizes, and budgets.

Episodic content transcends industries
Brands, regardless of industry, can create an original series for themselves. The more far-fetched, the better. From HR, to construction, to AI, to accounting, to IoT, to any other industry imaginable. The same way that you can create a TV show about any topic. If there is an audience for the topic, there is potential to entertain them; potential to create a show.

For example, let's imagine you and I run an executive coaching practice for SMB executives. We may have noticed in our sales process that CXOs are quick to shut us down, claiming "Oh I don't need coaching, I'm doing just fine!", but experience tells us that it typically does take them some time to open up before they reveal what areas in their work they need support in.

Based on this information we have about the persona and the culture, we get an idea for a show. We decide to create an original series around senior execs who *have* recently undergone coaching and share what learnings they've brought back to their brands.

We can create episodes around the areas of managing work/life balance, avoiding team burnout, motivating difficult employees, and so on. Nothing prescriptive, just conversations and ponderings. These episodes would be intended for our target audience to vicariously learn and get inspired by others like them who had similar stories and came out on the other side. Some of the episodes may get shared between friends, others may turn into sales enquiries. Most of all, if we're consistent, we stay top of mind for when they or someone in their circle does need something like this. We planted the seed, but it becomes their idea to reach out to us.

Episodic content transcends functions

Marketing is an obvious one. But beyond that, episodic content has practical, revenue-generating use cases for Sales, Product, and HR - among others. An organization selling a complex solution trying to increase product adoption and reduce churn may create an original series around creative use cases featuring 10 different brands for their product, end-to-end, to illustrate to existing customers the various applications of the solution they just purchased.

Consider Hubspot Academy. They've created sequential content that helps their users master the strategies, tools, and processes available within Hubspot and the greater inbound methodology towards making them great marketers. This is a great example of a product adoption use case (along with other benefits including introducing new marketers to the Hubspot ecosystem).

This can be led by the product team in conjunction with marketing. An organization looking to build rapport with a list of key accounts they hope to be in business with can create an original series around a domain that the decision-makers in those key accounts would be knowledgeable about and would enjoy riffing about - to shorten their sales cycles. For HR, to hit their headcount targets faster, they can create an original series showcasing their fun company culture as a cheesy 70s sitcom-style show featuring some of their best employees who appear for cameos. The only limit is your imagination, and probably your Netflix account.

Episodic content transcends company size
Whether you're a one-man band, a one-man department, or lead a multinational business, you can create your own original series. brands big and small have access to the same online distribution channels, the same customer dreams, fears, and curiosities that keep them up at night. Especially for SMBs, creating an episodic content series can be instrumental in building thought leadership and visibility, as we will soon discuss.

Small brands may have a certain vantage point that larger brands may not afford. For example, it could be the case that the smaller company is more nimble, more agile, spends more face-time with customers on the field, and so on. Such experiences grant them special insights that they can then use to tailor make a show. Comparatively, large brands that have been in business for longer may be able to address subject matters from a place of decades of experience (read: a place of *ethos*) reflecting on macro trends, or just creating content addressed to similar-sized enterprises, and so on. Regardless of how small or large a business is, tactical advantages can be found to create an original series.

Episodic content transcends budget

Probably best of all episodic content doesn't take much to get started, assuming you have a smartphone. In its humblest form, creating episodic content can be as simple as a one-man band whipping out their smartphones and starting to vlog at a regular cadence, as long as they brand their videos as episodes part of a series. Going a step further, a small startup may decide to grab two smartphones (or two DSLRs), some lav mics, and two tripods from Amazon to set up a talk show set inside their office. Larger brands can hire a video team to film a few episodes back to back in one day, and distribute them over a period of time. You get the idea. The beauty of this, especially for larger brands, is that it's not zero-sum. It can start at the grassroots level with one dude in his department on his smartphone. It's also great for personal branding, as we'll soon discuss.

Video content vs Original Series

Comparing generic video content and an 'original series' is the same as comparing a burger and a 30-day, dry-aged rib-eye steak. While both are fundamentally one of the same (beef), the latter is more *considered*, more artisan, more up-scale, and seeks to delight the customer with a compelling story they want to hear.

One of my favourite quotes which sit on my desk comes from Ira Glass, who said:

"Great stories happen to those who can tell them."

By choosing to create an original series, brands change the mindset of their customers along with it. All of a sudden, they're not just consuming another piece of content, they're now officially in for a treat. An original series feels like a chef-selected menu, something that was specially curated, created, and selected for an audience. This explains why online courses still sell in an age where there is an unlimited supply of free content. It's all because of how it was packaged.

Packaging *is* everything
How something is packaged affects our perception of it. I believe the quality of our ideas and content we create improves when we know that something is designed to be part of a select series we're creating. Original ideas for topics, questions to explore, and guests to invite surface. Show names begin to surface. Intro sequence, music, set design, and brand identity ideas all begin to surface.

We can invite our audience and customers into that state of mind along with us through how we communicate it online. When we first introduce our original series, we create buzz around it and celebrate it as such. By doing so, our audience will do the same. They go from "oh here's just another video" to "oh this is different, I want to tune in to this."

When you're done, you can publish your original series all across YouTube and social media.

Now that we've looked at what episodic content is, let's explore why there's more to it than meets the eye, and how it can hold tremendous value for your business.

3c. The Hidden Benefits of Episodic Content

There is more to episodic content than meets the eye. There are a lot of benefits that can be unearthed from following an episodic content strategy and building an original series.

Earlier in the book, we discussed the challenges content marketers face every day with balancing quality, frequency, and distribution all in lockstep. One of the overarching benefits of creating episodic content series is that it tackles all three of those effectively, as we will soon see. But first let me ask you:

What do you do with leftover roast chicken?

I'm hoping you don't throw it away. You and I know that there is so much that can be done with leftover roast chicken. But I'm no chef, so I googled it:

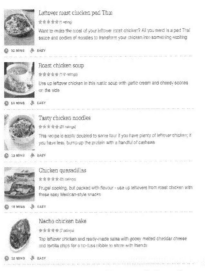

(source: BBC good food)

I don't know what time of day you're reading this, but it's 5:01 pm right now and this has definitely gotten me hungry. I digress, though this is a nice segway into the first major benefit of episodic content.

Content repurposing

The major, hidden benefit of episodic content is the ability to take each long-form episode and turn it into more video, audio, written, and even image content.

Think 1 episode = 50 pieces of content

This method of taking one video pillar and repurposing it was popularized in Gary Vaynerchuk's Content Model slide deck. It's an amazing resource and I recommend you check it out.

By creating your own original series, you set yourself up for success by repurposing each episode you put out into various content and microcontent pieces at once. This tackles the "frequency" piece. It's built-in.

This means that we can focus the majority of our time on creating quality episodes; the kind of episodes that we know we can extract more quality microcontent out of, in high quantities.

You can repurpose and get content from an episode in at least 7 different ways:

1. The full-length episode

2. Subtitled square videos for social (1:1 aspect ratio)

3. Subtitled horizontal videos for social (16:9 aspect ratio)
4. Subtitled vertical videos for social (9:16 aspect ratio)

5. Audio podcasts (isolating the audio from the video)

6. Written articles for web and social
7. Image quotes for social

All this can originate from a single episode.

Besides the fact that it is a blue ocean way of thinking that helps build brand, companies gain major efficiencies when they get their teams thinking in terms of episodic content as it holds massive repurposing benefits.

Episodic content helps to relieve the marketer burnout we have discussed earlier. By repurposing content multiple times per episode, you increase the shelf life, distribution, and reach of each episode (call it campaign if you like) without exerting additional effort in brainstorming and creating new content from scratch.

Everything is systematic. Everything originates from the pillar episode.

This improves the chances that the content will be seen, and all of it can then redirect back to the pillar episode (e.g: "click here to watch the full episode") or to a target URL pertaining to the campaign's goals.

"Series" signal quality

In 2007, Psychologist Barry Schwart presented an eye-opening TED talk titled the Paradox of Choice - his book of the same title. He explained why having too much choice can often be detrimental to our well-being, even leading to psychological distress. Choice overload, his studies revealed, can cause a lot of stress as people fall into a never-ending cycle of research, comparisons, and feeling of missing out and inability to make the "best" decision. Schwart reasons that by simplifying the choices we make, we can ultimately derive greater satisfaction from our daily lives.

Let's put yourself in the shoes of your customer, and apply that to content. When was the last time you were browsing the internet or social and thought "ah, I wish there was *more* content on this topic". Unless it was a genuinely specialist topic that's hard to find, my guess is: not that often. If anything, often times our struggle is having *too much* content to sift through. As a result, we find ourselves managing infinite open tabs and reviewing multiple content sources at the same time.

Make it exciting to binge-watch your content
By creating a dedicated "series" and packaging it as such, brands present discerning audiences with a curated, high-value selection of material that promises

to entertain as much as it will educate and engage. It signals a sense of quality and trust. It creates a platform for the culture surrounding a certain industry and connects the disconnected individuals over a common interest point. As they say, "it's not what you say, but how you say it."

Our content is at risk of being mistaken as me-too content if it's not packaged as episodic content, and part of a bigger, more integrated whole. As a result, creating an original series stands out as more polished, more organized, and ultimately - more attractive. Combined with frequency, credibility by association, and effective distribution - it cements mind share and thought leadership in the eye of your target audience.

Built-in frequency

With episodic content, the show must go on - by design.

As we will soon see, when brands plan an episodic content series, they begin with the end in mind. This way, the microcontent pieces from each episode are already planned - ahead of time. This helps them rest assured that for every episode recorded, it will create multiple content assets that are high value or high entertainment to their target audience, thus ensuring frequency of content just by adopting the episodic content mentality.

Further, it creates a feeling of constant momentum and continuity, that would keep their social calendars full and audience engaged.

They no longer have to worry about coming up with content ideas. Every time they need a new "idea", they simply create a new episode, following the overall theme and topic of the original series they created.

Incentivized distribution

Let's talk briefly about the elephant in the room that faces a lot of marketers, one that's close to a lot of hearts:

Will anyone actually see our content?
By 'anyone', we are referring to our target audience. Not our friends or ex-colleagues.
When you feature someone on your show, naturally they want to share that content on their own channels too.

To be sure, brands that build episodic series can set the expectation with their guests that this will be co-circulated on both of their channels (more on this later). Doing so ensures that not only will they get more reach and distribution (read: for free) but that the right people will see it.

For example, if you co-create a growth-focused show with Chief Revenue Officers (CROs), who then go on to share this on their networks - it is quite likely that they are also connected with other CROs, and other executives as well - who may pick this up and get to know about the show (and eventually, your business) through their contact sharing this content in the first place.

According to Jonah Berger in his book *Contagious*, one of the two top drivers of word of mouth are social currency (things that make us look good) and practical value (things that we believe will benefit others). Naturally, show guests may be motivated to share content that features them in a positive light, or features them sharing value that perhaps others may benefit from. Once it is shared, this can then repeat it self to the 2nd and 3rd degree level if their network are triggered the same way. All of this organic distribution compounds in your favour. We will talk more about how this can be designed, tracked and quantified later in the book.

Credibility By Association

For show types where you comarket with other influencers, brands, or generally having note-worthy guests on your show, you build credibility by association over time. This is a great exercise to show that you identify and share commonalities with them in areas such as:

- Points of view
- Level of knowledge
- Values and interests
- Willingness to help a certain group of people
- Level of trust
- etc

It's also a great discoverability engine for your business. For example, if you take the time to create a show and platform where guests on your show are Fintech influencers and experts, and you invite one of them to join - guess who will be the first person to share that content on to their networks? That's right.

Remember when we were saying that buyers are humans too? Same goes for guests on your show. In other words, if your original series did a good job of providing those guests with a platform to share their knowledge, views, or interests to an engaged audience, they will naturally feel inclined to share that content on to their networks.

Things like that hold tremendous benefit for B2B brands. We all understand the social credibility and trust that comes with someone else sharing our content and getting that earned media often outweighs what we share ourselves. Infact, 91% of B2B purchasers' buying decisions are influenced by word-of-mouth.

Reduce Costs Systematically

Traditionally, it's common for marketing teams to work in silos based on their function and skillset. For some brands, this means that the functions of video production, blog writing, graphic design, and analytics are often segregated - only meeting each other at team meetings. Sound familiar? This often results in duplication of work and hidden costs due to communication breakdowns, which cause additional friction and an overall disintegrated team.

By introducing episodic content to their teams, brands can reduce costs and free up budget to focus on what really matters - like building relationships with those who engage with the content - because everyone is aligned and motivated to think in terms of episodes. They understand that everything is integrated. They understand who is supposed to do what, when, and how.

It works like clockwork.

It brings teams closer when they realize that taking this integrated approach helps them support each other in meeting and exceeding their traffic and conversion targets month on month.

The team strategizes once, and deploys without friction in high quality, quantity and in multiple formats.

3d. Why Brands Can't Afford to Ignore Episodic Content

Creating episodic content is a mindset and strategy decision as much as it is an operational decision. By now we should have a solid grasp of several benefits that episodic content brings. But what can building an original series do for brands struggling to build (or defend) their brand?

1. An Unfair Advantage

Episodic content provides a proven methodology for growing an unfair advantage.

By building episodic content, marketers set themselves up for success by creating content that is simple to plan for internally but pretty complex for competitors to replicate due to the compounding of variables in their arsenal. Let's look at exactly why it provides an unfair advantage.

First-to-market
It matters whether a business is the first to create a show around their specific niche or focal point to become top of mind for their buyer personas. Personally, I do not believe you can run out of niches.

When a niche becomes mainstream, it creates opportunities to go deeper within that. With the right quality and consistency, this creates a true brand asset that holds attention and trust value that's pretty hard if not impossible to replicate exactly.

Guest relationships and selection
It is difficult to replicate the exact same roster of guests and re-create the exact same conversations and entertainment/education value. Not to mention, with each reputable guest and their klout score comes an added layer of complexity for competitors to match.

Multi-format content repurposing
By taking each episode and repurposing it for different social channels to create high volume microcontent pieces, brands create an act that's tough to follow. It also ensures that they have brand assets everywhere that their audience's attention is spent on. Whether that's on LinkedIn, Instagram, Quora, Spotify, or anywhere else. You no longer have to pick between "should we do a video" or "should we do a post". You can have all content types, everytime, because there's a process. Incumbents still working in silos will scramble as they experience burnout trying to match the quality and quantity of output you're doing.

ROI-centric

As we will discuss in more detail later in the book, by creating content pieces that are fully trackable and hold a dollar value, you make it easy for your department to show the value that marketing is contributing to the organization, in collaboration with other departments that are involved in the overall content-creation efforts.

2. Thought Leadership

Hubspot defines thought leadership as "building up a great reputation by giving your expertise away so that people think of your business first. It's about being the last word on a subject". A thought leader in business is someone (or some company) that constructively challenges the status quo with new vision, new information, or new methods to enable a group of people to do better work.

The great irony of many would've-been thought leaders is that they're too focused on their work to build the necessary brand awareness for it. On the other side of the coin, they may be keen to build brand awareness but have not yet discovered the right vehicle to enable them the spotlight that they deserve.

By building their own original series, brands equip themselves with a vehicle that they can use to curate and communicate with their target audiences the conversations, debates, questions, and findings that seek to stimulate and educate them - leading them to a new way forward.

This can be seen in documentary and behind-the-scenes style episodic series, where the creator brand starts with one question (commonly one that is important to their buyer) as they journey to answer it across a few episodes. This can be done in-house or in collaboration with guests that they meet on their way.

A great example of this is what Ernest Packaging did with their Cardboard Chaos Series. To answer their enterprise buyer's needs around the best quality packaging options, Ernest Packaging playfully demonstrated the durability of their cardboard by recreating every-day objects in cardboard. From cardboard guitars that they built for Linkin Park, to cardboard surfboards featuring pro surfers CJ Kanuha, Brennen Clarke and Jeff Deffenbaugh.

Rather than publishing a blog post, or even a video demonstrating the benefits of their packaging solution and their dexterity with customization - they drove the point home and built thought leadership by creating a dedicated original series. They continue to push the boundaries in every new episode they release.

Another superb example of this is Wistia's One, Ten, One Hundred series. In this series, Wistia sets off to answer one question - how much does budget play a factor in video production, as they recreated the same video for $1000, $10,000, and $100,000 respectively, presenting some surprising conclusions. By incorporating creative elements of storytelling, documentary-style shooting, and a razor-sharp understanding of their buyer persona, they were able to build thought leadership in that regard.

3. Personal Branding

Episodic content is a great way to build up the personal brands behind your small (or large) business. With this familiarity of faces breeds trust.

A note on trust

You and I already know this: people buy from people, not faceless corporations. According to Investopedia, a recent Harris poll reported less than 20% of people trust big brands in the banking, pharmaceutical health and health insurance industries. This trend is echoed in a study Ipsos released titled *When Trust Falls Down*, reporting that 42% of consumers claim to distrust brands, 69% distrust advertising, with 43% claiming that they trust advertising less than they used to. Most importantly, one of the key recommendations of the report is the call for brands to shift from story-telling to *anecdote-telling* - that is, "If you're a brand about thanking, how have you thanked? If you are a brand about sharing, how have you shared?"

A related HuffPost article captures the current sentiment among modern buyers perfectly:

"What matters [to millennials] is that they're not moved by flashy ads, big promises, and "wow" factor. They want authentic messages, authentic brands, and authentic interactions."

Ultimately, people trust people like them.

Build your personal brand, and theirs too
Episodic content and personal branding tends to go hand in hand. This holds true for "hosts" of your show, as well as any guests you invite on it.

When humans at a company "show their faces" in the episodic content they create, it builds trust. I'm getting to know you as a host, as a guest, as a person. Drift has a rule to never use generic stock footage in any content they create, and to lean on the true faces of their people, their customers, and their collaborators. Why don't you and I adopt that mantra too?

On hosts

A host may be the face of your company. It could be the CEO, another CXO, a manager, or an individual contributor in the field. The topic, context, or stance your show is taking on will help give you clues as to who is best suited to play the role of the host. One thing is for sure, they will be building their personal brand greatly by participating.

On Guests

Everytime you bring a guest on your show, you're contributing to the growth of their personal brand, and vice versa. Think about who would be the people best suited to feature in your content? Guests can be both internal or external, though often the latter. Mark Kilens, VP of Content at Drift maintains lists of people based on the expertise and context they bring, "I can then go back and pull from them based on the content we're looking to put together," he says.

In many ways, personal branding is the new branding because we trust people like us over faceless corporations. Episodic content is a vehicle for us to build our own personal brands inside the organization as well as lean on the personal brands of others who feature in our productions.

4. Staying Top of Mind

What do you think gets more word of mouth, Cheerios or Disney World?

In 2013 Jonah Berger revealed in his aforementioned book, *Contagious*, that one of the most important elements of driving word of mouth are *triggers* - that is when we're exposed to the same triggers over and over again, we are more likely to speak about them. This explains why Cheerios are much more talked about than Disney World, because we get a chance to see it every time we're at the supermarket. Disney World, even when it's more exciting of a topic, is not a day-to-day topic for most people.

Berger also observed that when NASA landed a rover on Mars and was enjoying great media coverage, Mars candy bars also experienced a spike in sales despite them not doing anything different - all because people were triggered when they were looking to buy a candy bar. The same can be said for content.

One of the most valuable things we can have in today's world is someone's attention. With all the repurposed content brands get from episodic content, they are able to continue staying top of mind by following a systematic way to creating engaging content across multiple channels.

Not every piece of content will necessarily be seen by everyone, but the *abundance* of content created will keep your brand and thought leadership top of mind for those with an interest in that topic and the value your company offers.

PART II:

"You can't build a reputation on what you're going to do."

– Henry Ford

4. Creating Your Own Original Series

4a. Understanding Different Show Types

One of the ways basketball players sharpen their skills after a game, during downtime, or before an upcoming game is by dedicating time to watching film, that is to watch basketball games with the intent of studying different player's movement, thought process, and overall style.

According to psychologists, the reason why this improves basketball player's game is due to something called Non-Conscious Behaviour Mimicry. This means that by watching something enough times, players begin to subconsciously copy what they see on screen - even without knowing it. This explains why oftentimes up and coming basketball players may have styles that resemble their favourite players - perhaps those they watch the most.

Same goes for creating an original series. By getting familiar with the different episodic show types out there and the purposes they serve, marketers can expand their vocabulary of creative ideas to put shows together that are both engaging as much as they are results-driving.

Before we start, a note on juxtaposition:

Juxtaposition, the secret to being interesting?
Juxtaposition is defined as two things being seen or placed close together with contrasting effect.

It is also a little-known ingredient in what makes shows stand out as engaging and entertaining - regardless of the show type.
That is - to take a formal topic and put a casual twist to it. Or to take a seemingly laid back topic and playfully make it more meticulous or formal. Other alterations include taking on taboo, elephant-in-the-room topics in an industry and addressing them head on with ease.

Similarly, using props to make the show more interesting. On the topic of props, here are three examples of props that can make any show instantly more interesting and therefore engaging:

The personality of the host
This one definitely plays a huge role. Not all hosts have to be picture-perfect charismatic, but it helps if there is a quirk about them that makes the episodes

altogether more interesting. This quirk can be that they are just truly and unapologetically themselves :)

Think about your favourite TV or online talk shows. Even in a standard talk show setting where the host asks the questions and the guest answers, I would bet that you follow certain shows not just for the guests they bring on but for the style and personality the host adds to the overall interaction.

It could be their interesting line of questioning.

It could be their ability to improvise on the spot.

It could be in the way they make the audience react or laugh.

Anyone can "ask questions", so it pays to really think about who will host your show.

In just a few pages we'll begin to learn more about different show (and host) archetypes out there, which will only highlight the importance of having a strong host.

A question we often get asked is whether a host can be outsourced. I'm not a fan. Why give away a golden opportunity to represent your own brand? Besides, it helps build the personal brand of that person especially if they are customer facing.

Hosts don't need to be picture-perfect charismatic as we discussed. Instead of being charismatic, they could also be highly credible, deeply knowledgeable, have an inspirational story, sarcastic, relatable, funny, even controversial - and so on.

The setting
Where and how you film your show matters. It's your job as a marketing to make sure of that. Ask yourself, is the setting playfully ironic? Is it interesting? Is it professional? Is it trust-building? Is it comforting?

Think of James Corden's popular Carpool Karaoke series being filmed in a car. You'd think that you'd want to have professional artists only sing in "professional settings" but the relatability of singing in the car is something many can relate to and provides just the right dose of quirky and remarkable. The setting and unique camera angles make it an instant hit.

Must all great shows be filmed in cars? Absolutely. Jokes aside, success here is how well you can convey the essence of the show through the setting you choose.

LinkedIn's Speaker Series show, where CEO Jeff Weiner interviews innovative thinkers and people with inspiring ideas, takes place in an intimate fireside chat setting with a small live audience. Do what works for your brand and get inspired by seeing other people's shows.

The objects in the room

Another clever way to build remarkability into a show is by the props and objects on set. This can be physical objects, can be the nature of the setting (as discussed earlier), something on the table, the way people are dressed, and so on. The only limit is your imagination, and the best way to train the imagination muscle is to not reinvent the wheel but rather to spend time studying other great shows (the more unrelated to your industry, the better) and what made them stand out.

Can a show be centered around a fun object?

Take the successful Hot Ones series by First We Feast- a show where they interview celebrities as they eat progressively spicier chicken wings, while answering equally 'spicy' questions, etc. The object of interest there is a row of delicious hot wings sitting between the host and his guests. Perhaps it's a blurred background of your office space which low-key showcases what your company looks like (assuming you have a cool office space).

One of the shows that I thought did this very creatively is RealLawyerReacts - a show where a lawyer in a dapper 3-piece suit reacts to legal scenes in popular Netflix shows as he watches them on screen to comment on their accuracy. In this case it's the 3-piece suit while watching Netflix. This nicely juxtaposes the laid-back idea of Netflix with the professionalism of being a lawyer, and so on.

Keep juxtaposition in mind when building your own show.

While one could argue there is a vast number of show types out there, in this book we will cover the 6 archetypes from where we can get a solid start to build shows and innovate further. Some of them may have elements that overlap, but ultimately each one stands out with its own set of unique advantages for your company.

1. Podcast Talk Shows

Definition: Talk shows are considered to be the OG of episodic content shows because of their simplicity and versatility. Talk shows are simply filmed conversations that take place between 1 or more [people] discussing topics, not unlike a radio or television talk show.

Many people commonly refer to talk shows as simply 'podcasts' as well. While talk shows classically started out as audio-only, here we examine them specifically as *video* talk shows. Filming talk shows allows brands to use this content and repurpose it across multiple formats beyond just audio.

Most commonly, talk shows tend to take place between 2 people where the host interviews, explores, or debates with the guest on topics that are meaningful to the intended audience.

It's worth noting that talk shows are not the same thing as customer video case studies, customer interviews, or customer testimonials. Talk shows are bigger than a company. Once again, they address a *culture* surrounding a specific niche or target audience you're serving. Some of the best B2B talk shows, while created by a brand, are in service to the people tuning in.

We can serve our audience using a mix of entertainment as well as education. It has to be gripping. Entertainment can mean inspiring, awe-inducing, exciting, suspenseful, shocking, motivating, and so on. It doesn't only mean "funny" or comical.
If you don't have any ideas yet don't fret; many of this stems from your topic and guest research as part of

your overall show strategy (more on that later). Talk shows can be the "town hall" meetings of your niche. Can you be the Larry King Live of your niche? Can you be the Oprah Winfrey Show of your niche? Think of it as almost as a personality test question. If you were a TV talk show, which would you be? We frequently recommend brands to use that as their muse and starting point to develop their own original talk show.

Example 1: #AskGaryVee Show (Gary Vaynerchuk)

One of the most popular personalities (and shows) among entrepreneurs and those with entrepreneurial tendencies. The description on their channel reads: "#AskGaryVee is the show, where I answer your questions about marketing, social media, entrepreneurship, and everything in between". It contains a mix of GaryVee on his own, GaryVee with guests, and GaryVee with multiple guests (panel discussions, see below).

Example 2: BrandWagon (Wistia)

Another instant classic original series from Wistia. The description on their channel reads: "From tactics to taglines, Wistia's CEO, Chris Savage, chats marketing with the brains behind successful brands.

Get a peek under the hood of their best campaigns, and watch as we spruce up an old station wagon along the way". Not only did they feature eye-opening conversations with global brand marketing heavy weights, they obsessed over all the small details of their production quality, storytelling, and banter to create a show that is equally entertaining as it is insightful.

Example 3: The Salesman Podcast (Will Barron, salesman.org)

A highly practical talkshow, The Salesman Podcast description reads, "The Salesman Podcast is the world's most downloaded B2B sales and selling podcast. Will Barron interviews the world's leading influence, body language, psychology and sales experts to give you the information YOU need to close more deals and make more money and really THRIVE in sales". Many of Barron's guests dial in remotely, which is proof that quality shows need not be done in person.

Talk Show Series Advantages: Talk shows have several advantages. One of the biggest ones is how easy it is for brands to get started with it. By simply selecting the right guests and preparing the right questions, creating talk show episodes enable brands to easily co-create the content through the conversations had with their guests.

A minimalist view to talk shows would infer that a host need only to come prepared with questions or topics for discussion, but the guest would provide the content. While that is true in principle, with the volume of talk shows out there today, that won't be enough. The more creative and well-thought our show can be - the better the chances of us standing out - unless you are one of the lucky ones to be able to pioneer the first talk show on your specific niche as discussed.

Another benefit of talk shows comes from distribution. By agreeing ahead of time with guests (or their brands) that the full episodes and the accompanying microcontent is to be co-circulated on both the host and the guests' social channels, the talk show can guarantee receiving a significant volume of targeted distribution among the right circles.

Borrowing from what we discussed earlier, another great benefit of talk shows is being able to build credibility by association. By having industry name brands, or people that already command the attention and trust of others on your show - you build this association naturally over time. By sticking to a certain caliber of quality in your shows, you begin to build thought leadership over time among the 1st and 2nd degree audiences you are reaching.

Things to keep in mind: Because podcast talk shows are very popular due to the low barriers to entry, it can seem difficult to create a show that would truly stand out. Luckily there are ways around that. Best practices include juxtaposing, going more niche, having an angle, or attracting a special caliber of sought-after guests.

2. Panel Discussions

Definition: Panel Discussions are a close cousin of the podcast talk show, but deserve a category of their own as they present a new dynamic format altogether. Panel Discussions are moderated by 1 or 2 hosts, and may feature up to 3-4 guests at a time. Panel discussions are great for brands who want to juxtapose different points of view to create for an interesting and valuable conversation for the audience. It is especially popular among disruptive technologies and service providers that may bring incumbents and new-age brands alike in the same room to explore certain topics and points of view.

Some variables brands can play on to make a panel discussion show interesting include company size, industry, domain knowledge (think old school vs new school), industry, or geography (and if your guests are only in town for a conference, grab them!).

Panel Discussion Advantages: One of the main advantages of panel discussions is the distribution multiplier effect - having multiple individuals participate in one episode likely means that it will achieve distribution across each of their respective personal networks and brand channels. This means being seen as a thought leader across a wider audience that is at the heart of your desired buyer persona. Absolute gold.

An additional advantage of panel discussions comes from FOMO. The fear of missing out on an episode where other competitors, influencers, or players in the industry will be speaking can drive influence. Similarly, they may attend the episode because they too wish to associate with others that you've invited, or perhaps they're looking to build a relationship with them as well. All these social factors are great ways to influence great minds to come together on your brand's show.

Things to keep in mind: Panel discussions don't need to dictate an entire show. For example, you may decide to have a podcast talk show, but one one or two of the episodes decide to turn those into slightly bigger panel discussions. You can also leverage the collective klout score of all the speakers at a panel discussion and turn that into an offline event to pull an audience. When selecting guests for panel discussions, make sure that your guests are comfortable with others who will be there as well, and that they know who will be attending.

If you're thinking of inviting high-caliber guests for your panel (as you should), make sure to plan well-ahead of time because getting three or more in-demand people to find a common time slot can be challenging from experience. Ways to overcome this can include making a mini-event out of it where it not only becomes a filming session for your episodes but also a networking/drinks event.

This gives them more reason to come, and gives you more of a larger pool of people to pick from in case there are any last minute cancellations. For example, you may choose to invite 6 guests to film two episodes with 3 guests each. Even if one cancels last minute, you can still have one episode with 2 and another with 3 - until you reschedule with the guest that could not make it. You get the idea.

Finally, panels should be fun and insightful, not intimidating. Make sure to do your research ahead of time to ensure that the guests and the topics will all be things that the guests will be ok with.

3. Reaction Video Series

Definition: People love watching videos of people watching videos or reacting to stuff. Who would've thought! Reaction videos are videos in which people react to events in general. You may have come across reaction videos of people reacting to music videos, films, games, or even reaction videos of people reacting to reaction videos. Before dismissing them as "fun-only" videos that wouldn't work for a business - consider the brands that leveraged the reaction videos phenomena and re-imagined them for their own industries:

Examples:

Example 1: Pricing Page Teardown (ProfitWell)

Profitwell, a SaaS subscription metrics platform, created a show where they react to company's SaaS pricing pages and reverse-engineer them. The description from their channel reads, "Pricing Page Teardown joins ProfitWell's CEO Patrick Campbell and Price Intelligently's GM Peter Zotto in tearing down pricing strategies from Netflix and Pornhub to Salesforce and Shopify using data collected from thousands of customers". Their content is entertaining, and educational.

Are you noticing a trend?

Example 2: RealLawyerReacts (LegalEagle)

LegalEagle is an online prep school for law students, created a show reacting to legal scenes in popular Netflix shows with commentary of their own. While not quite B2B, it's still a great example that provides a lot of lessons. A passage from his channel description reads, "I get asked a lot about whether being a practicing attorney is like being a lawyer on TV. I love watching legal movies and courtroom dramas. It's one of the reasons I decided to become a lawyer. But sometimes they make me want to pull my hair out because they are ridiculous".

What pop culture trends can your brand jump on to build a cultural connection while teaching them something cool?

Example 3: Allen and Lauri in the Morning (Sahouri)

Think insurance is boring? Think again. Sahouri, an insurance agency, created a show to react to and survey common seasonal hazards from an insurance perspective in a funny way. On their channel, the description reads, "Allen and Lauri is a web series covering CAI events, insurance trends and FAQ's for property managers and community associations."

What hypothetical situations are frequent in your industry that you can "react" to?

Example 4: Marketing Unboxed (Zaius)

Zaius, a B2C CRM, created a show reacting to a company's e-commerce campaigns and nurturing flows to pinpoint great tactics and ones that can be improved. Another great way of applying the reaction video genre to a business audience. Their show description reads, "Marketing Unboxed [is] Zaius' brand new video series where we dig into the marketing behind your favorite ecommerce brands."
What existing brands can you react to and create a series out of to entertain and educate your audience?

Reaction Series Advantages: There are three main advantages for brands leveraging reaction videos. The first one is the entertainment value.

There is a cool factor associated with reaction videos as it is part of an internet culture movement, and being able to bring that to an otherwise "boring" or "business" industry can be a great play to bring a fresh perspective (again, think juxtaposition). The second main benefit is that it is an indirect way to show expertise in a specific topic, by reviewing or assessing other things that are out there through the lens of your company's domain knowledge. Thirdly, reaction videos are unique in that they do not rely on having outside guests, and can be something that is taken care of by one or two employees internally in your company.

Things to keep in mind: Reaction videos can be quite effective when hopping on to current trends, other known brand names, or generally reacting to something that people already have prior knowledge about. In other words, it is not very effective to react to something that people don't know about anyway.

4. Documentary-style Series

Definition: Who doesn't like a good story? Documentaries for brands are not unlike documentaries that you'd see on your favorite non-fiction topics. A documentary starts with a key question, and sets off to answer it, on the way crossing paths with different characters, places, and situations on the way. The synthesis of different points of view, and different data sources in general - make it interesting for the viewer to tune in. This is one of the most natural and potentially cinematic experiences you can offer your audience.

Documentary-style series take a burning question, a pain point, or a point of immense curiosity, and send their team to go searching for answers for it. It may involve a medley of conversations with company employees, customers, prospects, partners, and other people that are relevant to participate. When done right, as with anything, it can be binge-worthy.

Examples:

Example 1: Wifinders (Mailchimp)

Mailchimp released a documentary series titled *Wifinders*. The show description reads, "Wi-Finders explores how easy access to the Internet has changed how people around the world make their living". From my observation, perhaps they recognized that many of their current or prospective users may be digital nomads, working remotely around the world from any location their heart desires on any given Tuesday. To that end, Wifinders chronicles some of these digital nomads' adventures.

What does this have to do with selling email marketing software, you may ask? Nothing, and everything. It shows that their brand is larger than life, and that they are attuned with the culture surrounding those original thinkers and courageous folk who rejected the status quo of working a standard 9-5 and opted in for something more exhilarating. Afterall, people don't by what you do, they buy why you do it.

Example 2: One, Ten, One Hundred (Wistia)

The debut show from Wistia, One, Ten, One Hundred is described on their channel: "In this Webby Award-winning documentary, we challenge a video production agency to make three ads with three very different budgets. With curious minds and a camcorder in tow, Wistia heads to L.A. to explore the complicated relationship between money and creativity". Deeply engaging and insightful, you not only get to learn so much about the relationship between budget and video production effectiveness, you build an emotional connection with Wistia as a brand, and what they do.

Random Thought: Can you build a show that makes people love your brand so much, they'd buy your T-shirts and Hoodies?

Documentary Series Advantages: Documentaries are one of those purist storytelling forms. They are great for fully immersing people into a topic that would matter to them. It definitely errs on the entertainment side vs. simply getting to the point - but the benefits of doing so is keeping your audience engaged for longer periods of time, and provides a piece of content that if well delivered, can be highly shareable among your buyer personas. A core advantage of documentaries is that they serve as timeless, "flagship" shows to establish thought leadership and domain expertise in the mind of the viewer.

Things to keep in mind: One flexibility this format provides is the ability to venture beyond what your company's day-to-day topics are - to tap into a wider topic with a wider audience. It may involve a higher level of production, which may be more costly that some of the other show types discussed here.

5. Behind-the-Scenes Series

Definition: Behind the scenes series are commonly company focused, and is a great way to make your audience feel exclusive - as brands tell a narrative of how their product, service, or other related component of your offering is made. More broadly - anything that tells a "making-of" or "exclusive" exclusive appeal can count as a behind-the-scenes series.

This insider-style content helps build relatability and affinity over time. This can be contrasted with "faceless corporations" that don't invite their customers for a look under the hood. Behind-the-scenes series are especially good if you have a large audience that's always been curious to get a backstage pass.

Alternatively, it could be great to chronicle the conception of a new product or service from start to finish. Similarly, it could be used to detail what goes in the creation of a final product, or even spotlighting some of the great people behind your brand. Even though this original series type may be a bit more company-focused than other parts, it's important to make sure that you're always answering in your mind the question of what's in it for the viewer from an entertainment and value-adding perspective. Is it funny? Is it educational? Is it inspiring? Does it tell a story? Does it involve other brands too?

Examples:

Example 1: The Game Plan (Spotify for Artists)

Spotify [for Artists] created The Game Plan, a show featuring Spotify insiders and successful musicians - from Rick Ross to Mike Posner - sharing tips with upcoming artists via Spotify. This is a "Behind the scenes" style show. Their show description reads, "Welcome to The Game Plan, a new series that gives you everything you need to get the most out of Spotify". Besides being a highly engaging show, it's also a great way to increase product usage with existing artists, which goes to show that original series can have benefits for departments beyond marketing (in this case, it's product and customer success).

Example 2: Cardboard Chaos (Ernest Packaging)

A great behind-the-scenes show example is Ernest Packaging which we covered earlier. Their show description reads, "That's what Cardboard Chaos is all about: taking on the impossible to show just how far packaging can go. Our cardboard guitar set the stage, and our cardboard drum has the crowd cheering for an encore. What do you think we have in store for the next act? You'll have to wait until the curtain rises on the next Cardboard Chaos!"

You indirectly learn about how durable their packaging is through the cool cardboard experiments they run - creating products for celebrities and making sure to film them test driving their products, from cardboard guitars, to surfboards and skateboards.
Pure gold.

If I or an organization in my network ever needs durable packaging solutions, I'll know who to call - by a landslide.

Behind-the-Scenes Series Advantages: Often synonymous with documentary-style series, behind-the-scenes series make your audience feel like they're right there with you, which just makes it easier for them to feel more familiar with your brand and what you're known for relative to others.

Behind the scenes videos also exude a level of confidence that your brand has nothing to hide, and on the contrary want to go deeper so that people really understand how you do what you do. It is also a great opportunity to showcase the personal brands of the individuals within your company, thus making it more relatable.

Behind-the-scenes series when done right, can also pose as a creative medium through which to co-create content with other influencers in your area, where you have them "feature" in different episodes or segments of your episodes based on where their experience or input will be relevant. This way brands can still leverage the benefits of distribution.

Things to keep in mind: To keep it engaging, behind-the-scenes series often involve a higher level of technical video production not limited to multiple camera angles, multiple settings, and multiple shooting-styles.

6. Live Talks

Definition: Live talks, like fireside chats, can make for great original series material. They can be intimate fireside chats, podcast talk shows, panel discussions, or even one-man speaker series done in a live setting. They have their own charm and come with their own benefits, and often suit brands that already have (or are planning) meetup events at a regular cadence. Breakfast series, monthly meetups, and other variations of company-organized networking events have the potential to become episodic in nature - if brands choose to package it this way.

Often, live events would settle for a 1-2 minute promo video. It's a missed opportunity. Why not record the full talks, package them as an original series, and repurpose them to maximize distribution and results? More on that later.

Examples:

Example 1: Speaker Series (LinkedIn)

What do Andre Iguodala (3x NBA champion), Barack Obama, and Sheryl Sandberg all have in common? They were all on the same show, along with hundreds of other notable figures in the worlds of business, tech, sports, and lifestyle.

LinkedIn's long-standing, multi-content Speaker Series is described by them as follows: "The LinkedIn Speaker Series is one of our favorite ways to support our mission of making professionals more productive and successful. We do this by exposing our employees and members to inspiring ideas and innovative thinkers from around the globe. The program also reinforces one of our core company values – that relationships matter". This show is filmed with a select studio audience, but is also broadcasted as episodic content on their platforms.

Example 2: Impact Theory (Tom Bilyeu, Impact Theory)

Not a traditional B2B show, but once again has immense learnings for those working in B2B. Tom Bilyeu is a successful entrepreneur best known for Quest Nutrition which he co-founded. His new company, Impact Theory, has a regular show which is described on their channel as, "Hosted by Tom Bilyeu, Impact Theory is an interview series that explores the mindsets of the world's highest achievers to learn their secrets of success". The fact that it is filmed with a live audience somehow adds to the intimacy and "realness" of the conversations. It is also one of my favourite shows to watch. I thought I'd add that!

Live Talks Advantages: One of the main benefits of live episodic content is being able to cocreate such content in the presence of a live audience. Depending on the format, Q&A sessions that follow after the main talks could also make for an interesting twist when planning microcontent. This has quality as well as distribution advantages. Further, being able to *episodically* wrap already-existing meet ups helps brands get two birds with one stone by capitalizing on events and getting more ROI out of them. This is especially valuable with event sponsoring, to extract more lasting value from budgets already committed.

Things to keep in mind: Because fireside chats and other live variations are happening "in the moment", all event management best practices would apply here. With context to creating an original series, it pays to obtain all necessary consent from your guests regarding topics that would be discussed, so as to avoid last-minute requests to *not* go live with certain content. It happens! Guests should be coming to your show with the understanding that any material shared will be repurposed and re-distributed online.

Now that we've covered the 6 archetypes of content shows, what's important is to just start with one, and pivot as needed. Iteration becomes easier when you have more historical data to go off of. When in doubt, consider starting with the "classic" podcast talk show.

Afterall…

"The worst of all human ailments: indecision"
 - Napoleon Hill

4b. Building Your Show Strategy

With today's technology, it's easy to put together different tools and processes to create an episodic series. Find the one that works for you. What you will see below is what works for us and our clients. Whether that show becomes a hit among your target audience or not depends largely on your show strategy.

Your show strategy foundation can be as simple or as complex as you choose it to be. Here is a simplified 8-step process that covers many use cases:

1. Defining your business goal
2. Selecting your target audience
3. Creating your show positioning
4. Planning topics
5. Selecting guests
6. Planning episodes strategically
7. Selecting your host
8. AV and Set Design

- ***1. Define your business goal***

Are you creating this show for thought leadership (marketing) or opportunity creation (sales)? Based on which you pick, you may prioritize which guests you bring on accordingly [more on that shortly]. Marketing goals can be measured in terms of traffic, leads, meetings booked, etc. Internally it could also be measured in terms of content productivity, and number of content pieces produced per month, quarter, and so on. Sales goals can be measured in terms of opportunities created, revenue-per-episode, and days to close. It is very important to choose a quantitative goal so it can be measured. If you're not comfortable choosing a fixed number, you can pick a range. It's important to apply the SMART methodology to goal-setting here, including:

Specific - A specific marketing and/or sales goal that you expect to reap from your original series. This also makes it easier to sell internally.

Measurable - This specific goal can be tracked as an objective and key result (OKR) or a business metric that holds bottom line value for your organization. For a detailed walkthrough on understanding and implementing OKRs, I recommend reading niket's Medium post titled *OKRs - The Fundamentals*.

Attainable - Do you have the resources and capabilities to pull off an original series of your dreams? Do you need to do a low-budget one with two iPhones to start, or are you going to hire professional gear, or perhaps a filming team? Do you have a plan to land the guests you're after? More on this later.

Relevant - Especially important if this is your first original series. Your goal from your first original series is to set a benchmark for yourself to beat. Think of it as going to the gym for the first time. You're not competing with the baddest body builder, you're just looking to beat your personal best over time. It can be tough to know what goal is attainable and what's not, so you can always treat your first original series (or episode) as a 'data-collector' or benchmark setter that will only improve with time. Once you start to gain momentum with putting out episodes, you can set realistic goals with your team to be understood by all. They have to be challenging, but realistic enough given your track record. You should aim for a 10-30% increase episode on episode.

Timely - You will need to set a due date for when your show will go live. Within that, you can set deadlines for when your show strategy will be complete, when your guest roster and timetable will be finalized, when the filming will take place, and finally when and how the content will be repurposed and distributed.

- ## *2. Select your target audience*

Who are you making this show for? Is it targeted towards decision makers right away? Or is it a grassroots-focused show, created to be shared among people in the field like individual contributors and line managers who will spread it on internally themselves? Perhaps it's designed to attract industry partners and distributors. Who is your show *not* designed for?

I was in IKEA the other day and saw a quote on their wall that read, "limited space brings out unlimited creativity". I saw that and thought this couldn't be more true of selecting a niche and sticking with it.

For the sceptics that thing niching can be selling oneself short, according to Ahrefs, 29% of keywords with more than 10K monthly searches were made up of 3 or more words. In the same research, 4 or 5-word phrases very commonly had more search volume than one or two word phrases.

Who is your specific persona and what are they searching for?
How can we select a show that will not resonate with everyone, but just enough with the right people that, as Seth Godin would say, *sneeze* it to their friends?

By making it clear who your show is *not* for, you make your target audience feel even more sure that this is definitely their jam.

In Daniel Priestley's book Key Person of Influence, he discusses the value of going niche, and how most brands today are global-ready by default. By focusing on a niche, while it may look small locally, globally it sets you up for success to be a big fish in your niche.

Here is a short passage from the book *From Impossible to Inevitable* by Aaron Ross and Jason Lemkin which perfectly captures the importance of niching, and orange unicorns:

"We are only gonna sell orange pens, special ones that draw unicorns. And we're only selling them to those brands who need orange unicorns drawn on their sales proposals in order to close big deals. Because we've seen that's where the growth is going to be, and we can be the best in taking advantage of it."

- ### 3. Create your show positioning

Nas has a lyric that goes:

"No idea's original, there's nothing new under the sun. It's never what you do, but how it's done."

It's not what you say, it's how you say it. It's the angle you focus on. It's the genre you do it in. It's the way it's presented. How will you make the show entertaining? How will you make your show the kind of production that people would enjoy (and gain from) tuning in to during their commute, on evenings when they're back home, or at work when they're pretending to work? Make sure your positioning is interesting and comes across as a breath of fresh air.

There are several devices at your disposal to easily achieve this.

One of them is juxtaposing as discussed earlier.

Secondly, you can look at Seth Godin's *Edgecraft* technique - being the most "something" at what you do. For example, the most in-depth, the most high-profile, the most credible, the funniest, the most honest, you get the idea.

Finally, a third device you can use is looking at a totally unrelated industry to see who is leading the pack there, the innovation they are doing, and seeing how you can copy that across your own industry. Think Henry Ford's assembly line (an innovation) being applied to sushi restaurants to enhance the experience and make it more word of mouth worthy.

Your show positioning rides on your company's positioning, but gives you room to iterate and embellish on it further to get even closer to your target audience and customers. It's important to recognize show positioning as one of the best ways to low-key express what your brand stands for, and a leverage to separate you further from the competition in a way that's too complex or sophisticated or nuanced for them to replicate. Invest time in this step to get it right. The best way to get something "right" is to ensure its aligned with your brand values and general positioning.

After that, comes planning topics.

- *4. Plan Topics*

Topic planning is a crucial step to building a successful business original series. The best combination of data collection here involves quantitative and qualitative methods.

Quantitative methods are important to understand volume of demand based on search results of where the attention is right now. YouTube videos often rank on Google Search prefixed at specific timestamps to answer a searcher's query. For example, I just searched for "How to re-construct flat boxes" and got a result of a YouTube video answering my question with a predetermined suggestion to start watching the video specifically at the 0:14 mark.

Quantitatively, you can use tools like Ahrefs, SEMrush, or just plain old Google suggestions (through autocomplete, or at the bottom of a search page) to understand topic volume, and also understand what topics are most in demand. You can also use a popular tool called AnswerThePublic.com to get inspiration on the types of questions people are asking online around your topic.

Qualitatively, you can organize an internal round table with your employees or interview Marketing, Sales, Support, or even your CEO on topics and areas they know are hot and in demand. If you have long-time customers that you can approach with their insights, that could be a valuable avenue to collect qualitative data as well.

It is very important that your show becomes culturally attuned to what your audience is looking for, and the qualitative element helps to balance that, and often gives insights into nuances that may be difficult to read from quantitative tools alone.

Loosely, each episode you design should focus on 1-3 topics. We'll talk about planning sub-topics per episode shortly. Your initial goal should be to end up with a list of 10-12 topics or questions that are quantitatively and qualitatively verified. Those will be worth crafting episodes around.

- **5. Select Guests**

If topic planning is the yin, guest sourcing and selection is the yang. The next step in creating your show strategy is to make a list of possible guests that could be great fits for the topics you've identified.

Make sure that this is aligned with your goals. If your goal is to get maximum reach, accelerate warming up your target accounts, or something else - this should have an influence your guest selection. Two general things to keep in mind when selecting potential guests for your show are their online social influence and relevance to your goals.

Online social influence refers to their followership on relevant platforms like LinkedIn, Instagram, and Twitter (to name a few), whether they work for a company with many employees (read: distribution!), or generally regarded as an influencer or authority in their space.

For relevance to business goals, make sure to review the first bullet point to make sure your guests are aligned with that. If you're looking to boost sales by co creating a show with target accounts, have you verified internally if you are doing outreach to the right people?

If you're looking to build a show to generate highly relevant traffic back to your website, have you taken into consideration the guest's klout score and 2nd degree network quality?

If you're looking to build credibility by association, have you studied the guests' achievements and track records to ensure they're a good fit for your brand and what you stand behind?

Equally important is your relationship with those guests. Are they 1st degree contacts, or are they in your extended network. If the former, great! If the latter, how best can you plan a warm intro to them? Make sure that when teaming up guests to episode topics that it plays to their strengths and their sweet spots so that they are at ease.

Asking yourself these questions early on during the show strategy phase helps you save valuable time later down the line.

- *6. Plan episodes strategically*

After you've matched your yin with your yang - or the right topics with the right guests, the next step is planning the sub-topics within each episode. Brands that do this ahead of filming their episodes have the benefit of knowing what the microcontent will shape up to look like.

This means that they're going in knowing that they will be filming "quality" episodes packed with entertainment and utility, and not leaving it to chance - which quickly becomes a waste of everyone's time and money.

Brands that plan their episodes strategically know what subtopics to go after which would in turn represent individual or multiple content pieces. Some of your show guests who may like to prepare may ask you to send them a copy of the questions you intend to ask.

While you may not send them the exact questions, you made share with them top level to subtopics you intend to cover. Aim to plan 5 subtopics per episode at the minimum. This means you can at least get 5 microcontent clips from each episode. It's always important to align on this so that the episode is repurposable.

Finally, planning episodes and topic guides ahead of time helps especially if you're preparing this for someone else who will play the role of show host. Speaking of which...

- **7. Select your host**

Who will be the host of your show? For SMBs, this is often the founder, CEO or a CXO. For larger brands, it may also be a CXO, but often times is also a Director, VP, or star rep (i.e with a certain personal brand). These aren't hard set rules, just trends some of the aforementioned brands tend to follow.

Depending on the show type, you may also decide that different line managers or individual contributors may step up to the plate as well to simultaneously help with the content creation process while building their own personal brands. You can also look at others in your space as well as shows in unrelated industries to get inspiration. Really the only limit - besides your business goals - is your imagination.

When looking at different hosts, here are some host types to give you a sense of the tendencies of each profile. Personality and style (e.g: charismatic, funny, serious, casual, formal) are not factored here.

The high-level host

This could be a CXO, VP, or Director. They're interested in the industry as a whole, trends, and predictions. Super powers include being a veteran of the industry, and having an ability to identify with similar senior execs with ease.

The technical host

They could be a senior manager, individual contributor, or anywhere in between. They're interested in going in deep on specifics, tactics, and take a more operational focus. Super powers include being great at uncovering actionable value that can be applied right away, but also do it with flair and relatability.

The curious host

This could be anyone at the organization. They're curious about finding answers to a question through conversation and research. It may be about a topic they are openly exploring with the viewers, or a new area that the company wants to build influence in over time by leveraging the experiences of others. Super powers include being great at asking insightful questions, and maintaining an open mind.

Finally, comes:

- ## *8. AV and Set Design*

Last but certainly not least, is where your show will take place and how it will be filmed. There is plenty of content out there on how to DIY a video podcast setup, from 2 iPhones, to DSLRs and lighting kits, to hiring a video production team for the occasion. Having said that, going into detail on how to pick and set up cameras and microphones is beyond the scope of this book. Nevertheless, here are some things to keep in mind:

Use the best you have
When it comes to video, I love what film director and YouTube influencer Casey Neistat said in his YouTube video titled *How to Vlog like Casey Neistat by Casey Neistat*, which is to simply use the best gear you have access to at any given time. This can be anything from one smartphone camera, to hiring a professional video team. Having worked on all of these with clients before, the simple conclusion for us was to keep it consistent.

Keep the filming consistent [per show]
Your AV setup needs to be consistent so it looks the part (no pun intended). If a show is filmed on

smartphones, then it's smartphones all the way. Abruptly upgrading the footage a few episodes in may disorient the viewer, versus picking a standard that you stick to. If you're going to get it professionally done, stay true to that too.

The good news for us is that we're not bound to stick to one set of film gear or even one filming style (let alone show type). Every new show brands create is a new, open canvas and opportunity to revisit their AV set up.

When we were starting out, me and my co-founder Aamen filmed our very first podcast show (spareroom talks) in a spare bedroom in my apartment, where we shot on two android smartphones and a GoPro hero 5 Session mounted on tripods. It wasn't much, but it had a consistency to it. We practiced and learned so much in that show, and you will too from your first one. Luckily, we've upgraded equipment since!

Great audio is everything

Next comes audio. I personally believe that great audio literally makes a video look better. The good news is that investing in decent mics doesn't need to break the bank.

With decent lavalier ranges starting at just $20, and upwards from there. At the time of this writing, one of our budget-friendly favourites is the Audio-Technica AT2020 which is a condenser mic.

Finally comes set design. Put simply, you need to plan the setting where the show will take place. Naturally this can be a room in your office, your co-working space, or a venue rented for the occasion. Sometimes brands we've worked with have also leveraged on-going events (like conferences) to film and source guests there. If you already have a branded recurring event of your own such as a meetup or breakfast series, then you can certainly skip the queue and leverage that.

On Set Design

Set design here simply means the look and feel of where your show will be filmed. Can we find a cool spot in your office to film? If opting in for a meeting room, will there be any props to make it more interesting for the viewer? Will you go for natural lighting or hire a lighting kit? Draw inspiration from your favourite talk shows, stages and events to see what elements you can draw together for your series. Consider also what we discussed around juxtaposition earlier as that could help here.

On Post-Production

Polish up your full episode after filming. Some bare essentials to consider:

- Color correcting the footage so that it looks warmer
- A short 2-5 second graphic/animated intro and outro
- Lower thirds (graphic overlays) to introduce your guests
- Your branding/logo throughout the episode

4c. Distribution and Repurposing

Planning and filming original series is only one third of the game. The remaining two thirds are finding the answers to these questions:

- How many people will see this?
- How many people will engage with this?
- How will this generate measured results?

Enter distribution and repurposing.

If we ~~build~~ film it they will come, right?

I'm not going to lie, I've definitely seen it happen. For most of us though, it genuinely comes down to how much distribution and repurposing went into it. Let's tackle distribution first.

Co-Distribution is the new distribution (say what)
We have to be creative and resourceful when it comes to distribution. There's no nobility in sharing branded content *only* on our company channels.

Infact, prior to taking the show assets live (whether full episodes or microcontent), resourceful brands map out *all* the relevant stakeholders from both their own and the guests's company. Especially with the guest's company (if they invited guests on the show), they make sure everyone anticipates, plans, and executes on co-distributing the show.
Does this sound self-serving? Not really. Let me explain.

When done right, it's highly possible that your show provided a platform for your guests to share their wisdom, insights, and stories. The guests should generally see the benefits of co-distributing this content as it helps them convey their thought leadership through their own personal channels as well as the companies they work for where relevant. Furthermore, it compounds the organic distribution effect, and drives success all around. An easy way to operationalize this is by sending an email. Here is a template you can tweak:

Hi [show guest],
Thanks again for joining us on the episode! You added a lot of value in the areas of X, Y, and Z which I think our joint audiences will appreciate and engage with.

Our goal is to make sure as many of the right people as possible see this episode and subsequent microcontent that will come out of it. To do so, we want to involve as many relevant people from our company as well as yours to participate in sharing the content on to their own networks, as it may start multiple valuable discussions. Would you be able to connect our marketing team with yours, I have them copied to this email. Separately, let me know if there are any other key individuals or teams from your company that you'd like us to send a copy of the completed assets to.

[Your name]

Here is another template you can modify and send to your own team:

Hi team,

As you know, we are planning the launch of our new original series titled XXX. It will add a lot of entertainment and utility value in the areas of X, Y, and Z which I think our audiences will appreciate and engage with. But I need your help.

Our goal is to make sure as many of the right people as possible see the episodes and subsequent microcontent that will come out of it. To achieve this, we're relying on you to participate in sharing the content you like on your LinkedIn, as it may start multiple valuable discussions.

[Your name]

Here is a list of people to aim to get on your "distribution" map both internally and externally to share the content:

- You!
- The host
- Your marketing team members
- Your sales team members

- Your leadership team members
- Your customer-facing employees
- The guests
- The guests' marketing team
- The guests' leadership team*
- The guests' customer-facing employees*

understandably easier said than done. The more interesting your show is the more naturally this will occur, though.

You must celebrate

Celebrate that you have a new show! Don't permit it to fall on deaf ears. Make sure people are excited about it. Get teammates and your greater community involved with pitching future episode ideas. Make them owners in the process. Explain to them that it can only be successful if they partake in spreading the word. They can easily make it their own and enhance their personal brands (even if they were not involved in the show) by adding their own context; writing their own captions.

The case for repurposing

A 2019 study carried out in the Technical University of Denmark found that global attention spans is getting narrower and that trends don't last as long as they used to.

"Content is increasing in volume, which exhausts our attention and our urge for 'newness' causes us to collectively switch between topics more regularly," commented Philipp Lorenz-Spreen of Max Planck Institute for Human Development - as cited in The Guardian article covering this research.

So how about that 30 min episode we just finished? Fear not. Long-form episodic content will always appeal to a section of our audience. The same way some of us like to watch entire games and others like to tune in to the highlights. There's always an audience for both. Often times one begets the other. By repurposing content into smaller, microcontent pieces - you appeal to a wider demographic within your target persona.

"Is lasagna just spaghetti with cheese?"

This was a real question posted on Quora.

The answer is no, it is not.

Not unlike the relationship between lasagna and spaghetti with cheese, microcontent offers fundamentally different value from the original [pillar] episode, to different audience types with different preferences. The one thing they all have in common is that they share an interest in your content. This is why it's important to increase the shelf-life of your original series by taking steps to repurpose the content.

Some people may prefer to listen to the audio podcast version of your panel discussion while driving home or at the gym. That's how they stay productive and get in the zone while on the go.

Some people may prefer to read a summarized article of what took place in the episode because that's how they focus and take notes, or share concise info with colleagues at work.

Some people may prefer (expect?) to see your content in the form of subtitled video microcontent on LinkedIn as they go about checking their phone in the lift or on the computer with audio off.
Some people may love to know the absolute key take aways in the form of poster quotes celebrating the best one-liners from the episode.

By the way, just because they saw the poster quotes doesn't mean they won't go back and watch the episode. As discussed, the microcontent can also serve as teaser content to drive attention to the full episode. Alternatively, it could be used to drive traffic back to the call to action you have set for them.

People have attention spans that aren't getting any longer any time soon, and repurposing is how you stay flexible amidst that.

10x the return on each episode created

How can you get more than 10x the value of each episode you create? If you've went through the work of putting complete episodes together using the guide in this book, you can leverage each video episode to create [more] video, audio, written, and image content. Smaller snippets of content of the greater "pillar" episode is what is referred to as microcontent.

I. Subtitled microcontent videos

For video content, one thing you can do is create microcontent from the sub topics discussed in each video episode. You can create horizontal videos and square videos using video editing software on the market today like Adobe Premier, Final Cut Pro, or Davinci Resolve as well as online cloud video editors. By uploading the clips to YouTube, you can get them "auto" subtitled, and through extracting the (.SRT) files and importing them into your video editing tool of choice you can burn the captions directly onto the video, or even upload the file separately on LinkedIn and Facebook when posting, which will automatically overlay the subtitles at the right time. You can also use paid services like Rev.com or HappyScribe.com. Keep in mind that any "auto-subtitling" solutions out there may require editing too based on nuances in pronunciation, industry terminologies, and so on.

You can experiment with:
- horizontal videos and square videos
- subtitle fonts, sizes, and styles
- social media captions (e.g: bold statements vs discussion questions)
- Hashtags
- Tagging others who are relevant to the video content*

The guests should most definitely be tagged. This is in reference to 3rd parties who were not present at the interview but may find the content useful or interesting or may wish to add their ideas too. Social media is still the party of the internet.

II. Audio

For audio content, you can use audio editing software to extract the audio from the episode and export it as an mp3 or high definition WAV to syndicate across to SoundCloud, Spotify, iTunes, Stitcher, and other podcast platforms. Take the time to edit out the umms and ah's to polish it up further. Consider removing parts that don't add to the final result or have no relevance to an audio-only medium. Consider also adding a dedicated podcast intro and outro which makes your audio-following feel heard (no pun).

III. Written Summary Article

For written content, you can get into the habit of condensing the concepts that were discussed in each episode to produce a written summary. Some people also like to add show notes or provide a text transcript for the conversation that took place.

Personally I value seeing dedicated articles that riff on the episode in a new way, as opposed to simply recording the conversation. If I needed a transcript I could have watched or listened to the episode. In other words, it's always good to approach articles as if they are standalone content pieces in and of themselves.

You will find that every microcontent piece should be stand-alone in quality in and within itself.

IV. Poster Quote Images

For image content, you can pick 1-3 memorable quotes from each episode that you decide to posterize by creating a quote design. Those can be distributed as horizontal or square poster quotes for various platforms. If you're stuck for design, grab one from Canva. Keep it simple!

Second Reminder:
I know I said this before, but I need to stress this, as it's a core success factor for your episodic content. Before taking any content live, make sure to liaise with your guest(s) and their brands' marketing teams where applicable so that they're *in* on what's going on.

This way, they proactively post or reshare the content you create once it's taken live. You both get free distribution and social credibility in one. You can easily drive commitment by sharing this information ahead of time in an email or nicely branded PDF plan that becomes a standard process for your company.

Tracking results and ROI

What really brings original series full circle is closed-loop reporting. According to Hubspot, closed-loop reporting is in essence getting sales to report on the effectiveness of the leads generated and delivered by marketing to determine actionable insights based on what worked well and what can be learnt from.

Consider this journey:

- Target account A that you're after is invited to an episode on your show
- The episode is developed and co-distributed along with microcontent
- One of the video microcontent pieces piques the interest of someone in Target account A's network who then visits your website, starts a chat, and books a meeting to speak with your sales team
- They become a customer

Stuff like this happens all the time but can be difficult to attribute. I think us marketers will forever be trying to one up our current attribution efforts. At my company, we adopt a purist, first-touch attribution mentality. To track results, I suggest creating tracking links per microcontent piece, per channel.

By creating tracking links per microcontent piece, per channel, we quickly develop a deep understanding of where the attention is coming from. We structure the tracking links to factor in topic, medium, and format.

This way we are able to capture insights across all three fronts. We don't just want to know that a microcontent video on the topic of say "shortening sales cycles" got a lot of traction - we want to know that it was the square video that we ran on instagram vs the square video we ran on LinkedIn, Facebook, or Twitter that got the most traction.

Similarly, we want to know that the article we posted on medium drove more traffic or leads than the article on our own website. Here's a simple breakdown:

Unique Tracking Link =

- Destination URL
- Social Channel
- Content Type
- Content Title

Destination URL - that's your call to action. It could be your homepage, landing page, a link to the full episode, the article write up to it, or anything else you deem fit.

Social Channel - LinkedIn, Facebook, Twitter, Soundcloud, Medium, Quora, Instagram (link in bio)

Content Type - full episode, microcontent video, image, story, article

Content Title - Name your microcontent pieces so that you know what they were about when you're looking at the data. For example "What I learnt about raising capital"

To construct the tracking link using the above elements, you can use whatever tracking link tool you already use, including Google's free UTM tracking link builder - or grab a free template from tribetactics.com. Ideally the final link can be shortened using a service like bit.ly or Rebrandly.

Measuring ROI from content doesn't need to be complex. The law of diminishing returns kicks in pretty fast once you're already doing some basic best practices. Whether you're using Google Analytics, Hubspot, Buffer, bit.ly or other tracking tool - the essence of tracking is the same:

- Measure the attention you're getting online, and from what sources

- Understand the quality and quantity of that attention
- Applying insights to your next campaign (or episode) to keep growing

From my time working at Hubspot as an agency marketing consultant, I learned firsthand that analytics can be as sophisticated as you'd like it to be. For the purpose of this book as discussed we'll take a purist approach to ROI tracking. Here is what you need:

1. A tool to create tracking links per content piece
2. An understanding of how much 1 lead is worth to your business.
3. A feedback loop between sales and marketing, and marketing leadership and marketing to communicate what are the most result-generating content pieces, in order to do more of what works with each episode.

You can quantify how much 1 lead is worth by:

1. Starting with your average sale value
2. Calculate your close rate % (e.g: maybe you close 1 in 10 opportunities you have that's 10%)
3. Calculate how many leads it takes to create one opportunity or SQL (e.g: for every 30 leads 1 becomes an opportunity)

Based on this simple funnel, you should be able to estimate the value of each lead to your business. Use tracking links to understand which microcontent pieces drove the most traffic to your website, chatbot, form, free offer, enquiries form, or anything else that you measure. You can then go a step further by checking for trends across topic, format (video, audio, etc) , and medium (LinkedIn, Facebook, etc) as discussed.

Now you are ready to build your brand's original series. You know how to plan, execute, distribute, and track the return on your episodes produced.

Now we are ready to get a tad bit more advanced. In this section, we will learn how to leverage our original series to build true thought leadership and drive new business.

"Do not follow where the path may lead. Go instead where there is no path and leave a trail."

– Ralph Waldo Emerson

5. Building Thought Leadership With Your Original Series

One of the critical differences between creating ad-hoc videos, and other content pieces is the aspect of continuity that series have. Specifically, continuity around a specific topic that you can build association and thought leadership with over time.

Credibility by association

It can be hard building thought leadership without many years of experience in a certain field. As Priestley said in his book *Key Person of Influence*, "you are who Google says you are". By co-creating content with others who are leaders in their field, you build credibility by association. Beware that as this approach becomes more and more popular, brands will have to come up with more novel angles and ways to ensure that they have their audience's attention and ultimately trust.

It's not enough to simply copy and paste this approach you have to be attuned to the culture.

Always remember to create content for the culture

Take the concepts in this book with a pinch of culture. People see right through gimmicks. It's important that you make sure that you create content that is 'current' with how people in your industry think such that it becomes relatable and easy for them to engage with. Is there an elephant in the room? Is there a general concern around a certain topic?

Is there a trend going on that people are still trying to figure out? Consider building an FAQ of topics prevalent in your industry's culture to help you prioritize the narrative that would be most effective to adopt. From there you can apply some of the devices discussed in this book such as juxtaposition to find an interesting angle that makes it binge worthy.

Connect and Champion New Views

One of favorite books is Shoe Dog by Phil Knight. In it the founder talks about his journey building Nike from scratch. Along with his fellow co-founders, Knight was an athlete runner and admired other star runners. One of the early success factors, back when they had no brand, was to sponsor runners most likely to win because they believed they also embodied key attributes of the Nike brand. In turn, it made it easier for people to 'get' what Nike stands for.

Fast forward all these years, it flipped. Today, athletes getting associated with Nike know receive similar recognition benefits. Who can you associate with who already embodies and champions the worldviews, attitudes, and beliefs you have? Those are the people you need to bring in to your show. It makes it easier for you to be understood. It makes it easier to add value to others because you made it easier for them to relate to you. You may even look outside your industry for inspiration and contacts. Think about it, and you will know when you meet them.

"No one is useless in this world who lightens the burdens of another."

– Charles Dickens

6. Generating New Business With Your Original Series

When you go to a bank, you cannot take out money from your current account that was not already there to begin with. Similarly in sales, today more than ever, you cannot extract value without first giving it upfront.

It explains why cold outreaches and other traditional forms of business development are decreasing in popularity and effectiveness. Where did you add value to me before asking for some in return?

In Adam Grant's book *Give and Take* (one of my top 3) his research reveals that most people are marchers. That is, most people are happy to give value so long as they expect to receive that value back - and vice versa. A huge part of value adding in sales comes in the form of building relationships. They say you should build partnerships not clients. With that in mind, utilising your original series as a platform to meet and co-create value with people you hope to partner or be in business with is a very natural way of building relationships that can be streamlined as a step in your opportunity creation pipeline.

No hard sells. Just relationship building and mutual value creation. The worst case scenario is that you'll get a lot of great content out of your episode to grow your brand awareness. That's the worst case scenario! The best case scenario is you identify opportunities to add value to one another.

The Content Distribution Advantage

One of the greatest benefits of having target accounts and potential partners on your show are the networks they have. If they don't do business with you, it may be that one of their industry peers who's a similar persona to the one you're targeting comes across one of the articles, microcontent videos, or image quotes featuring their contact which in turn piques their interest in you.

Don't be surprised if they reach out directly with an enquiry, or to ask for an opportunity to feature on your show.

The Relationship Nurturing Advantage

For those of us in long sales cycles, it pays to have a streamlined mechanism to build relationships while co-creating value. Such content may be seen by others working at their company who may be future decision makers or users of your offering.

Our world is made up of mini tribes and the more people you tap into the more circles you get access to if at least on a 2nd degree level. Always remember Google's Zero Moment of Truth research that we discussed earlier - that it takes 11 touchpoints, 7 hours, and 4 different methods for people to go from awareness to making a purchase decision. Having said that, I cannot stress enough the importance of being genuine and courteous in your approach.

There is a thin line between being interested in someone for the value they can add to a conversation and for them to think this is a ploy. Take care of this one thing and everything else will fall into place. Remember Dale Carnegie's famous saying - that you can make more friends in 2 months being interested in them than in 2 years trying to make them interested in you.

Measuring ROI and Insights

As with everything, it is important to make sure that this is a cost effective use of your time and your team's time. Going to the gym can be a waste of time or a life saver, depending on how you use it. Make a commitment to yourself as a leader and with your team that you will start building original series, but be objective with how much you put in and what you get out.

It's never too late to pivot to a different audience or a different angle. A classic A/B test you can try is to create one show for decision makers, and another for users - to see which one gets more traction. Collect insights from every episode and share it with your team. I recommend monitoring:

- What worked
- How (quantitative - measured in traffic, leads)
- Why (qualitative - measured in topic, medium)
- What didn't work (quantitative, as above)
- Why (qualitative, as above)
- Next steps for next episode/show (based on learnings)

<>

At this stage you may be feeling a little inspired or even raging to get an online original series going. Only one thing may stand in your way, buy-in. If you work with people, you need to sell them on your vision to stakeholders to ensure that they can join you in championing and executing on this.

This is what we will discuss in the final section.

"The best way to predict the future is to create it"

– Abraham Lincoln

7. The Business Case: Getting Buy in Internally

Do you remember the quote I told you about that sits on my desk? Here it is again: "The best stories happen to those who can tell them".

Communication tips from Wolf of Wall Street
In the movie The Wolf Of Wall Street, there was one scene where Jordan Belfort (played by Leo Di Caprio) brings in Steve Madden (played by Jake Hoffman) to speak to the stock brokers about his new product in hopes of motivating them to sell more of his company's stock.

Within seconds of starting he gets booed off stage. Belfort joins Madden on stage to settle down his heckling crowd of stock broker employees. He then proceeds to tell facts more relevant to what they care about. How he's a visionary, someone to watch, and someone that should interest investors. Someone that would be easy to sell because of the public growth of their brand.

"This is our golden ticket to the f***ing chocolate factory right here!"

He got them fired up and ready to do just what he needed them to do - sell Steve Madden stock.

Say what you will about this movie, but once thing is true - telling stories that people want to hear is powerful.

When it comes to selling the vision you have for your original series, your pitch will change depending on who you are speaking with, and what's important to them. In the book *The Challenger Sale,* Matthew Dixon suggests that people don't take action in business unless there is a [big] problem that drives them to find a solution. Otherwise, why rock the boat? Why do anything for that matter?

a. Top Down: Convince your team

If you run a marketing team at your company, it's important to get your team members buy in. An easy way to do this is to involve them as early as possible in the ideation and brainstorming process. It's important to explain to them what's in it for them - namely, that they would be able to get more out of every content piece they produce in a fraction of the time.

Rather than working with an agency or other outsourced team for strategy, your team can keep all the credit by following the episodic content framework. This means that they can streamline their work and align around creating pillar episodes from which all the content originates. It also means they can put their creative hats back on again (isn't that why we all got into marketing?) and be more strategic with content creation, upcycling and repurposing as they go.

Ensure an objective criteria when building your original series with your teammates. Make sure it is aligned with your business end goals. It may not be a bad idea to buy this book with them too (shameless plug).

b. Bottom Up: Convincing leadership

This is where most of us may live. Now that you have your hands on this book and even have a working title or concept for a show, how do you build internal buy in? It's all about speaking in terms of their own language, and at tuning your pitch to what matters most to them. Depending on who you report to (CXO, VP, Director, or Manager) the pitch may change slightly.

However, common themes and challenges here include:

Sales

- Hitting revenue goals faster
- Shortening sales cycles
- Creating an additional pipeline for warm leads

Marketing

- Building thought leadership
- Improving lead/MQL quality
- Increasing traffic
- Increasing content without increasing headcount
- Improving relationship with sales
- Avoiding employee burnout/turnover
- Standing out from the crowd
- Working smarter not harder
- Building domain authority in a new sector

As you reach through those, you may find that some are more aligned with your internal priorities than others. Anchor your pitch around those.

Episodic content and building original series should come out of a business need as opposed to a nice to have, because it is. Especially if the status quo is not working out as everyone hoped it would.

You stand the opportunity to help reframe the conversation for your team and your organization to help everyone become more productive and successful.

c. Grassroots: Do it yourself

Whether you're a marketer or sales person, you can leverage the concepts from this book and apply them to your own personal brand on LinkedIn and other social networks to start a mini series with yourself. All you need is a smartphone and a lav mic from amazon for $20.

Sometimes the best way to make a point, or advance an idea, is to put it in practice yourself and wait for everyone else to see its positive effects. You have the power, so why not do it? Sometimes this mini series can get you new job opportunities, make you more valuable as an employee, as well as get you meetings with senior people at your company so they can get your advice on how they can do something like that for their own brands. The only limit is your imagination.

8. Behind-the-Scenes Chat with Mark Kilens, VP of Content @ Drift

I sat down with my friend and former colleague Mark Kilens, VP of Content and Community at Drift. Before Drift, Mark spent eight and a half years at HubSpot, starting as an Inbound Marketing Consultant and growing his career in marketing along the way leading up to becoming the VP of HubSpot Academy, which he created - working long evenings and hours for months on end.

"At the beginning of 2019, I joined Drift to work on a holistic content strategy for the entire business. Not just for marketing and sales, but for customer success, the entire business, and work and lead all of the community efforts, including the HYPERGROWTH events we do. So that's what I do now. I'm really excited about content, obviously."

I thought he'd be the perfect person to flesh out some of the ideas discussed in this book further. We had a great conversation, which we transcribed and reproduced for the book below:

1. On scaling content creation through others

Kareem:

You've seen so much. One thing that I wanted to ask you is, how can a brand leverage their community to scale content creation?

Mark:

I think content is a core part of your demand gen and growth engine. Marketing has two goals, to drive growth and build enduring brands. That's the job of marketing, and to do that, you need content today more than ever. Content is not something that's been recently created. It's been around for a long time. It goes back 100+ years.

Think about how much content you create on a daily basis. And this could be shared personally with friends, family or whomever else publicly. You could do it through various social platforms as a person, at a personal level, or coming from you as someone who works at a business creating content. And most importantly, you don't have to be in marketing to do that. A ton of salespeople now use content to get their message out.

Customer success teams in software and service businesses should be empowered to put out more content these days. It would be foolish, almost irresponsible if a business doesn't empower and leverage all the people in its community.

So for me, I think of how to do this as a business, and it starts with leveraging everyone — from employees, your team, to customers, partners, and even prospective customers and buyers to get them to create content with you.

If you think about it, they're already doing it. You, as marketing, need to be the broker where you bring those people together and define a goal the content is trying to achieve. It goes back to what you are trying to do with your content to create more awareness and grow top-line revenue.

From there, the question then becomes what content would you create and how would you go about creating it? I think of that as four elements.

1. *Why* would you create a piece of content?
2. *How* would you do that with people in your community?
3. What *types* of content would you create?
4. *Who* would you involve?

2. Not involving others in content is irresponsible behaviour

Kareem:
Going a bit deeper, how would we go about featuring, not just customers, but even our own employees? How do we go about operationalizing that?

Mark:
The first thing I would do is identify the people that are most active in the ecosystem. You first start by creating a list of folks, and as you then come up with ideas for content, you can pull inspiration from that list. I have lists of people from different personas, which is another way you can do it. You can also do it by type of person. I do the same thing with our employees.

Mark:
After compiling the lists, I look at it with my team and decide, for example, "here are the people that have expertise in these things," and "here are the people that have a lot of opinions and points of view about these other things." There are five or six lists that I have, and I can then go back and pull from them based on the content we're looking to put together. You can track the relationships you have with those people. I'd keep track of things like whether I have been introduced, how many conversations I've had with them, or perhaps when was the last time I spoke with someone.
Mark:

It's important to get very detailed around actually knowing who you are speaking with. You could use any of the free CRMs out there to easily organize this with your team too. Organizing people in that way will then help you as you go through your cadence of building each show or episodic piece of content. Know that you have this population to reach out to and pull from.

Mark:

I would do that well in advance. At the end of the day, you have to build relationships with people. You can't just ask them for something, typically, unless you have a very, very strong brand. If you know you want to have someone on your show, down the road, say it's in three months, build that relationship three months before. I think that a lot of people fail to do that, Kareem. They don't actually warm up the person, and they also fail in reciprocation — that is, "I've got this great thing from you, what can I do for you?"

Mark:

It has to be a two-way thing. You just contributed all this amazing value, how could I help you or your business, now that you just gave us an hour of your time to be on this show? Reciprocity is one of Cialdini's principles of influence. We should remember that reciprocity is the key.

Kareem:

Couldn't agree more. I love that you make internal lists of people, and it can be an easy way to build relationships cross-departmentally. In sales for example, it would be "who would have an opinion on how things are right now?" How can we get them involved? And so on.

Mark:

100%. I have these lists right now. And again, it depends on the size of your business, but if you have a couple of hundred people at your business, you should make these lists. As a content marketer, get to know every new person who joins the business, somehow. Your goal is to build relationships with people and to share their knowledge, stories, and experiences.

Kareem:

I'm noticing an ongoing theme in our conversation, which is that marketing should play the role of becoming a facilitator of content, and shift away from the mindset of "only marketing creates our content". You mentioned it earlier, that it's almost irresponsible for others *not* to be participating in a company's content efforts.

Mark:

Definitely. That's exactly what I did at HubSpot. That's exactly what I'm doing at Drift now. That's what I'll do for the rest of my marketing career. And that's how you grow an enduring brand and get your whole company to do marketing with you, other than just promoting your stuff. Make them part of the marketing experience and the brand experience, not just promoting a thing we just published. That's not the right way to do it.

Mark:

The right way to do it is to include them. As a marketing team, you will never have all the knowledge or all the answers or all the information. You should rely on your community — the three or four groups of people that we already talked about in your community to give you that knowledge to then help you grow the business.

3. Building trust in a skeptic world (Pt. 1)

Mark:

People have less and less trust with organizations these days. People are more skeptical than ever before.

Kareem:

I think we were talking about this topic separately, that people trust other people as opposed to companies.

Mark:

Yes and people usually trust people more than organizations. So then if you can have your voice or your content come from people instead of the organization, you have a leg up, I think.

Kareem:

Absolutely.

Mark:

And that's why almost all the pieces of content that we create at Drift, we include quotes from people, based on the person we're targeting with that content. So if I'm writing a piece for CMOs as I did recently, I'd include five quotes from other marketing leaders and CMOs in the piece.

Mark:

Or it could be like what Dave Gerhardt does with Marketing Swipe File, which is an episodic show where he has marketing leaders, and even sales leaders and other types of people in that marketing show. Then you can use that in other pieces of content. So I think, getting back to the diversity of thought, those people don't have an agenda. They very unlikely have an agenda. As a business you naturally have an agenda.

Mark:

That's another reason why you want to include your community. You're naturally biased, trying to drive growth and turn a buyer into a customer. You might say things in a way that don't resonate well, as opposed to someone who naturally has fewer biases.

Mark:

Everyone at your company is hopefully pretty bought into what you do. The mission, the purpose, and how you're going about what you're doing. Other folks might not share that same feeling but some folks will. So get those people who are excited and passionate to share why.

Mark:

So again, there's that authenticity in what you're then creating, because it's coming from their voice, assuming of course you don't try to massage or refactor the content they share with you in a non-genuine way.

Kareem:

Yeah, totally. On a related note, we're building a new show at the moment that I like to think embodies that. It's a motivational original series with some of the local heroes of the Dublin tech scene capturing their untold stories, valleys they had to endure, and their spirit of perseverance and chasing their dreams. It's called The Warm Intro.

Kareem:
I think it plays to what you said, which is really the importance of creating content genuinely for the culture. The culture that you're part of, the communities that you're part of. We didn't want to create a show to say, hey, "buy our products". It's more like, "Hey, we all have to work hard and persevere in the face of failures, here's a series with people who've been there and done that."

Kareem:
An outsider may not be sure how this relates to what we're doing or selling. And maybe there may not be a direct correlation there, but ultimately we're trying to tell a broader story in hopes that it would resonate with the types of people we hope to build relationships with down the road. Perhaps the show can act as a platform for them to start conversations when they're going through challenging times, or winning mindsets to adopt.

Kareem:
We hope that celebrating values like that will pay its dividends towards our brand awareness down the line. Perhaps it's not as direct as people would think. But, we do believe that something like that would be of value to create. I know this is something that Drift does an amazing job of.

Mark:

Yeah, that's exactly what David Cancel and Dave Gerhardt did with Seeking Wisdom.

Kareem:

Yeah, exactly. I love that show. Which at a glance, may not *directly* relate to what you're doing, but ultimately some way, somehow, will add collective value to everyone involved.

Mark:

Yup, yup.

4. Building trust in a skeptic world (Pt. 2)

Kareem:

We talked about featuring guests on shows. How do companies actually go about making them the star, but in a way that is genuine and not forced or generic? After all, it's the right thing to do, plus we know audiences can instantly tell the difference.

Mark:

I believe preparation comes first. You have to do prep and make sure they understand what you're asking them to do and why. I think a lot of people forget the *context* when working with people to create content. I always make sure that the person who I'm working with is getting the context.

Why are we doing this? How is it going to be used? Why are we asking you to do it? Why do we think you're awesome? There's a lot of context there. I even sometimes tell people, here's why we're asking folks that are outside of Drift to create this type of content with us. We really give them the whole story, which also contributes to building trust, doesn't it? Any good leader gives great context. It brings clarity, and clarity trumps persuasion. Clarity is really important in communication, so as you communicate with these people and prep them for the content, it will probably make what they tell you that much more compelling.

I was just talking to a CMO about their experience with Drift. I think she's seeing a lot of success, and her team is seeing a lot of success with Drift. We had a great conversation. I think we built a lot of trust and that now I feel very confident that's going to turn into a long-term relationship.

I asked her at one point in that conversation like, look, I'd love to have you share what you just shared with me with others, because of these reasons. Here's why I'd love to have you share this. Here's what I can do for you, because of this. I asked her, "what else could I do for you?" How else could I help you? So that the reciprocity is felt.

Another point to highlight is that people all have a sense of self-esteem. How do you appeal to that in some way? We can convey to them that, "look, we want to tell your story, and we want to tell this part of your story, and we think it's super interesting. We think our community [don't even say buyers and customers], is going to be attached to it; fascinated by it."

And also, as you do this, explain to them that this is going to come out at a specific time. Set the proper expectations; it's going to be a month out, three months, whatever. It doesn't have to be right away. And "we'd love to have you participate in sharing with your community too, your network. Because at the end of the day, this is not about us. This is about you."

Make sure it's about them, not you. That's super important. Make it about them, not you, and you'll get more of that.

So, yeah, I think those are some simple ways. Maybe not all simple, but those are some ways that you can make them more the star and make them feel special when they're creating content with you.

Kareem:
Completely. We have a variation of that where we say, let us not make it about you or me, let's do this for our joint community. We often try to prep them up in a sense that we always think of our joint end community and how best we can add value to *them*, in addition, of course, to making sure that the guest is naturally the star.

Kareem:
We talked earlier about the reciprocity piece being key from Robert Cialdini's book [Influence]. But at the same time as well, you're going into depth, which is where the genuinity piece is, highlighting why you think you'll add so much value, and how you're super keen on contributing back, in exchange for your time, or for your insights during this period, and so on.

Mark:
I actually think it's multiple Cialdini's principles. The reason you also make the customer the star is like authority. They are the authority. They're social proof. There's reciprocity. There's liking. Those are four of the six right principles there.

5. On getting off on the right foot

Kareem:
We've covered a good few things today. For someone who's never done any of this before, what is a good framework to approach what we discussed?

Mark:
Start with your customer success team or sales team. It could be one person running customer support or success. It could be tons of people, but regardless, they have relationships with customers. Ask those people to introduce you to some customers that they feel are seeing success and are happy with your product or service and are excited and have them make introductions to you.

If you don't have that type of business model, go on social media. Find the people that are excited about your product or service and reach out to them. Say something like thank you so much for your support and advocacy, we appreciate it. It's incredible. I have something to ask you though. Would you like to do something with us? Oh, and by the way, if you did this, it would be published in this thing.

Mark:
It doesn't have to be customers, just people in the community or at your organization. I do this for my partner team all the time. I did this with our partner team at HubSpot. You were on the partner team, Kareem. Think about how many partners were featured in our content.

Think about what Kevin Dunn did, think about what Kevin Dunn is doing right now with an episodic show.

Kareem:
Yes, Agency Unfiltered.

Mark:
That's a great example. Those two things to getting started. And always ask yourself,why? It goes back to your content brief or content plan or your show strategy to decide who would be a good fit.

I'm always a person who starts with a goal and then ask why. Why are we doing this? Next, we find the people to reach out to. You could do it the other way as well though,because you need to build a relationship with these people after all. You can't just be introduced and be like I have an ask.

Sometimes it's better to go and build these relationships with a couple of people, knowing that in a month or two, you're going to need to ask them for something, because you have this piece of content you want to create that's episodic or short-form episodic content. Those are the two easiest ways to get started.

Finally, it's just making sure you keep track of all of these things you're doing with people. Again, CRM, spreadsheet, whatever tracking or project management software such as Trello, Monday.com, or Asana. But regardless, make sure you track the relationships, as it helps you make sure you understand what's going on.

Those are the things that I think are most important to do to get started.

<>

9. Conclusion + Final Thoughts

I want to tell you about some of my favorite films and what they have in common. Oceans 11, The Godfather, and GoodFellas. They're all about an inside circle of well connected professionals that have an alliance that cannot be broken. Each of them is spearheaded by a thought leader who calls the shots but also looks after everyone else. I've always been fascinated by this concept. Building enough relationships and thought leadership to have special access into circles like that. Building shows is a great first step to helping you surround yourself with people smarter than you are, who can add to your business while you simultaneously help them back and grow your own influence as a business, or as a person.

This book was written across many countries and many devices (including 1 phone which I lost and replaced with another - thank god for Google Docs and Evernote! It's travelled with my as I finished compiling it across Dublin, Rotterdam, Amsterdam, Krakow, Athens, Santorini and Crete.

My only hope is that you enjoyed this book and found inspiration in some way shape or form. Perhaps it even gave you an idea to start an original series for your brand.

Even more so, I hope in it you found all the reasons why it's never been more important to really build and cement thought leadership using episodic content, this amazing, timeless format. I also hope you found in this book the starting strategies, processes and tools you need to get it off the ground.

As a thank you for making it to the end of the book, if you're stuck with any questions or want to brainstorm ideas for kickstarting your own series, repurposing the content, or getting internal buy-in, I'd be delighted to hear from you and help in any way I can. My email is kareem@tribetactics.com.

I look forward to binge watching your new original series - across video, audio, written, and image.

Warm regards,

Kareem Mostafa
Co-founder @ tribetactics

Acknowledgements

Thank you to the tribetactics team- for your support in building the dream!

Thanks also to our friends who've supported us with their insights and contributions, Mark Kilens, Chris Savage, Dave Gerhardt, Irina Nica.

Thanks also to our first show guests Hesus Inoma, Hongbo Sun, Thomas Arnold, Iliyana Stareva, Garret Flower & Daniel Paul, Conor McCarthy, Yasmin Vorajee, Rory Kelly, Sharen Murnaghan.

Special thanks to everyone else who has been cited in this book for your ideas, inspiration, research, and breakthroughs.

Thank you to Stephen Bergin.

Thanks to all our friends in the Dublin tech and startup circles including Hubspot and our community at Huckletree D2 and Shoreditch (Aislinn Mahon, Lauren Burgess, Bryan McGarrigle, Evan Lundgren, Eamon Cullen, Ciara Smith, Amanda Houlihan and the rest of the gang. You know yourselves!

About the Author

With today's technology and access, anyone can write and publish a book. I'm no best-selling author, just a fellow practitioner who noticed something great brands do and decided to write about it.

My name is Kareem Mostafa and I'm an Egyptian living in Dublin, Ireland. Along with Aamen Mostafa, I am a co-founder of tribetactics, a platform that helps brands create original series and repurpose existing episodes into tons of microcontent pieces month on month to save time and grow revenue systematically.

Before tribetactics I've worked at marketing agencies and understood what it's like working in the field. I've spent years working in a tech startup (which I co-founded), which taught me a lot about the challenges early stage brands face which is a clever way to say I learnt a lot from my failures.

From there I transitioned into the corporate world. I've worked in operations at LinkedIn for several years where I helped support the launch of the Middle East and North African markets (spanning 20+ countries). During that time, I set up an evening marketing consultancy after hours through which I delivered workshops to tech startups to audiences in diverse cities like Dublin, Amsterdam, Berlin, Lisbon, and Porto. From there I joined Hubspot where I trained under some of the best marketers. I received a world class training on inbound marketing in Boston. My role as a Partner Marketing Consultant consisted of advising over 80 different marketing agencies across Europe, the Middle East and Africa as well as some of their direct clients on how to attract, engage and delight customers online through inbound marketing. I've delivered international workshops to Hubspot user groups where I got to spend more face time with agencies and brands anywhere from 2 employees to 1000+ employees.

During my studies, I've completed a marketing dissertation on the factors that trigger word of mouth in online communities, and studied business, marketing, and entrepreneurship across the Emirates, Ireland, and Canada.

When not working, I spend my free time planning trips with my wife, playing music, visiting family, and hunting new restaurants spots with my brother and co-founder Aamen. Oh and of course, thinking of new series ideas!

References

1. "Video Will Account For An Overwhelming Majority Of Internet Traffic By 2021". *Business Insider*, 2019, https://www.businessinsider.com/heres-how-much-ip-traffic-will-be-video-by-2021-2017-6?r=US&IR=T.

2. "Three Myths Of The "67 Percent" Statistic". *Siriusdecisions*, 2019, https://www.siriusdecisions.com/blog/three-myths-of-the-67-percent-statistic

3. Pink, Daniel H. *To sell is human: The surprising truth about moving others*. Penguin, 2013.

4. Hintz, Lauren. "What Is The Buyer's Journey?". *Blog.Hubspot.Com*, 2019, https://blog.hubspot.com/sales/what-is-the-buyers-journey.

5. "Content Marketing | Definition Of Content Marketing By Lexico". *Lexico Dictionaries | English*, 2019, https://www.lexico.com/en/definition/content_marketing.

6. Tate, Ryan et al. "Tabloid Chic: How Racy Headlines Unlock Money And Power". *WIRED*, 2019, https://www.wired.com/2013/02/tabloid-chic-the-rise-of-racy-headlines/.

7. "5 Data Insights Into The Headlines Readers Click". *Moz*, 2019, https://moz.com/blog/5-data-insights-into-the-headlines-readers-click.

8. Patel, Neil. "5 Characteristics Of High Converting Headlines". *CXL*, 2019, https://conversionxl.com/blog/5-characteristics-high-converting-headlines/.

9. Bernazzani, Sophia. "What Is A Pillar Page? (And Why It Matters For Your SEO Strategy)". *Blog.Hubspot.Com*, 2019, https://blog.hubspot.com/marketing/what-is-a-pillar-page.

10. "Why 3000+ Word Blog Posts Get More Traffic (A Data Driven Answer)". *Neil Patel*, 2019, https://neilpatel.com/blog/why-you-need-to-create-evergreen-long-form-content-and-how-to-produce-it/.

11. Smarty, Ann, and Ann Smarty. "How To Turn Your Old Articles Into Successful Long-Form Content". *Coschedule Blog*, 2019, https://coschedule.com/blog/long-form-content/.

12. Howells-Barby, Matthew. "The Anatomy Of A Shareable, Linkable & Popular Post: A Study Of Our Marketing Blog". *Blog.Hubspot.Com*, 2019, https://blog.hubspot.com/marketing/seo-social-media-study.

13. Sailer, Ben, and Ben Sailer. "How To Write White Papers People Actually Want To Read (Free Template)". *Coschedule Blog*, 2019, https://coschedule.com/blog/how-to-write-white-papers-templates-examples/.

14. Winn, Ross. "2019 Podcast Stats & Facts (New Research From June 2019)". *Podcast Insights*, 2019, https://www.podcastinsights.com/podcast-statistics/.

15. "Self-Directed Learning From Youtube - Think With Google". *Think With Google*, 2019,

https://www.thinkwithgoogle.com/intl/en-ca/advertising-channels/video/self-directed-learning-youtube/.

16. "Apple'S Podcasts Just Topped 50 Billion All-Time Downloads And Streams". *Fast Company*, 2019, https://www.fastcompany.com/40563318/apples-podcasts-just-topped-50-billion-all-time-downloads-and-streams.

17. "14 Visual Content Marketing Statistics To Know For 2019 [Infographic]". *Venngage*, 2019, https://venngage.com/blog/visual-content-marketing-statistics/.

18. "Why We'Re More Likely To Remember Content With Images And Video (Infographic)". *Fast Company*, 2019,

https://www.fastcompany.com/3035856/why-were-more-likely-to-remember-content-with-images-and-video-infogr.

19. "Five Statistics About Infographics | Progressive Content". *Progressive Content*, 2019, https://www.progressivecontent.com/blog/five-statistics-about-infographics/.

20. Cialdini, Robert B. *Influence*. Vol. 3. Port Harcourt: A. Michel, 1987.

21. Tow, Hannah. "39 Important Branding Statistics You Have To Know In 2019". *Learn.G2.Com*, 2019, https://learn.g2.com/branding-statistics#b2b.

22. "Why B-To-B Branding Matters More Than You Think". *Forbes.Com*, 2019, https://www.forbes.com/sites/mckinsey/2013/06/24/why-b-to-b-branding-matters-more-than-you-think/#7ab3666259dd.

23. "25 Branding Stats & Facts That Will Change Your Life". *Lucidpress Blog*, 2019, https://www.lucidpress.com/blog/25-branding-stats-facts.

24. "7 Surprising Stats About The Underappreciated Power Of Thought Leadership". *Business.Linkedin.Com*, 2019, https://business.linkedin.com/marketing-solutions/blog/linkedin-news/2018/7-surprising-stats-about-the-underappreciated-power-of-thought-1.

25. "2016 Content Preferences Survey: B2B Buyers Value Content That Offers Data And Analysis". *Demandgenreport.Com*, 2019, https://www.demandgenreport.com/resources/research/2016-content-preferences-survey-b2b-buyers-value-content-that-offers-data-and-analysis.

26. "8 Dangers Of Growing Your Business Too Fast". *Inc.Com*, 2019, https://www.inc.com/cox-business/eight-dangers-of-growing-your-business-too-fast.html.

27. "Every Fast-Growing Company Has To Combat Overload". *Harvard Business Review*, 2019, https://hbr.org/2016/06/every-fast-growing-company-has-to-combat-overload.

28. "Council Post: 15 Signs You're Scaling Your Company Too Quickly". *Forbes.Com*, 2019, https://www.forbes.com/sites/forbescoachescouncil/2018/03/05/15-signs-youre-scaling-your-company-too-quickly/.

29. "Great Companies Obsess Over Productivity, Not Efficiency". *Harvard Business Review*, 2019, https://hbr.org/2017/03/great-companies-obsess-over-productivity-not-efficiency.

30. "The State Of Brands Taking Marketing In-House, In 5 Charts - Digiday". *Digiday*, 2019, https://digiday.com/marketing/state-brands-taking-marketing-house-5-charts/.

31. "SWOT Analysis For Advertising Agencies". *Bizfluent*, 2019, https://bizfluent.com/info-8463866-swot-analysis-advertising-agencies.html.

32. Watson, Leon. "Humans Have Shorter Attention Span Than Goldfish, Thanks To Smartphones". *The Telegraph*, 2019, https://www.telegraph.co.uk/science/2016/03/12/humans-have-shorter-attention-span-than-goldfish-thanks-to-smart/.

33. "18 Moments To Explain Why You Should Post 100X Per Day". *Garyvaynerchuk.Com*, 2019, https://www.garyvaynerchuk.com/create-content-100-pieces-per-day/.

34. *Contentmarketinginstitute.Com*, 2019, https://contentmarketinginstitute.com/wp-content/uploads/2017/09/2018-b2b-research-final.pdf.

35. "The State Of Content Marketing Survey 2017 | Zazzle Media". *Zazzle Media*, 2019, https://www.zazzlemedia.co.uk/resources/state-content-marketing-survey-2017/.

36. "85 Content Marketing Statistics To Make You A Marketing Genius". *Optinmonster*, 2019, https://optinmonster.com/content-marketing-statistics/.

37. "2019 Marketing Statistics, Trends & Data — The Ultimate List Of Digital Marketing Stats". *Hubspot.Com*, 2019, https://www.hubspot.com/marketing-statistics.

38. "2019 Marketing Statistics, Trends & Data — The Ultimate List Of Digital Marketing Stats". *Hubspot.Com*, 2019, https://www.hubspot.com/marketing-statistics.

39. https://contentmarketinginstitute.com/2017/10/stats-invest-content-marketing/

40. Sinek, Simon. *Start with why: How great leaders inspire everyone to take action*. Penguin, 2009.

41. "2019 Marketing Statistics, Trends & Data — The Ultimate List Of Digital Marketing Stats". *Hubspot.Com*, 2019, https://www.hubspot.com/marketing-statistics.

42. "Data Talks: Proven B2B Lead Gen Tactics - Marketo". *Marketo Marketing Blog - Best Practices And Thought Leadership*, 2019, https://blog.marketo.com/2015/08/data-talks-2-proven-lead-generation-tactics-to-jump-on-now.html.

43. Hintz, Lauren. "The Inbound Sales Methodology". *Blog.Hubspot.Com*, 2019, https://blog.hubspot.com/sales/inbound-sales-methodology.

44. "75 Remarkable Sales Enablement Statistics". *Lotops*, 2019, https://lotops.com/75-remarkable-sales-enablement-statistics/.

45. "What Happens Online In 60 Seconds? | Smart Insights". *Smart Insights*, 2019, https://www.smartinsights.com/internet-marketing-statistics/happens-online-60-seconds/.

46. "Internet Statistics & Facts (Including Mobile) For 2019 - Hostingfacts.Com". *Hostingfacts.Com*, 2019, https://hostingfacts.com/internet-facts-stats/.

47. "One Thing Is Killing Content Marketing And Everyone Is Ignoring It". *Content Marketing Institute*, 2019,

https://contentmarketinginstitute.com/2017/02/killing-content-marketing-ignoring/.

48. https://trackmaven.com/blog/marketing-leaders-strategy-technology-data/

49. "We Analyzed The Sales And Marketing Practices Of The Top 100 Saas Companies. Here'S What We Found. | Drift". *Drift*, 2019, https://www.drift.com/blog/cloud-100-2018/.

50. *Forbes.Com*, 2019, https://www.forbes.com/cloud100/#718f2185f941.

51. "Dukecmosurvey-Measuring-Biz-Impact-Social-Mktg-Spend-Aug2016 - Marketing Charts". *Marketing Charts*, 2019, https://www.marketingcharts.com/business-of-marketing-70233/attachment/dukecmosurvey-measuring-biz-impact-social-mktg-spend-aug2016.

52. "Leftover Chicken". *BBC Good Food*, 2019, https://www.bbcgoodfood.com/recipes/collection/leftover-chicken.

53. http://www.usefulsocialmedia.com/brand-marketing/how-social-media-amplifies-power-word-mouth

54. Reporters, Marketing. "Why Silos Are The Enemy Of Effective Marketing – Marketing Week". *Marketing Week*, 2019, https://www.marketingweek.com/silos-enemy-effective-marketing/.

55. "Close More Deals With Sales & Marketing Alignment - Marketo". *Marketo Marketing Blog - Best Practices And Thought Leadership*, 2019, https://blog.marketo.com/2016/04/dynamic-duo-close-more-deals-with-sales-and-marketing-alignment.html.

56. Visaggio, Maggie. "What The Heck Is Thought Leadership Anyway?". *Blog.Hubspot.Com*, 2019, https://blog.hubspot.com/marketing/what-is-thought-leadership.

57. Pollitt, Chad, and Chad Pollitt. "How AI Is Helping To Reduce Waste In Digital Advertising". *Social Media Today*,

2019, https://www.socialmediatoday.com/news/how-ai-is-helping-to-reduce-waste-in-digital-advertising/525980/.

58. Hobbs, Thomas. "Marketers Continue To 'Waste Money' As Only 9% Of Digital Ads Are Viewed For More Than A Second – Marketing Week". *Marketing Week*, 2019, https://www.marketingweek.com/2016/07/26/marketers-continue-to-waste-money-as-only-9-of-digital-ads-are-viewed-for-more-than-a-second/.

59. "2019 Marketing Statistics, Trends & Data — The Ultimate List Of Digital Marketing Stats". *Hubspot.Com*, 2019, https://www.hubspot.com/marketing-statistics.

60. "B2B Content Marketing 2017 - Benchmarks, Budgets & Trends - North Ame...". *Slideshare.Net*, 2019, https://www.slideshare.net/CMI/b2b-content-marketing-2017-benchmarks-budgets-trends-north-america/1.

61. "How To Avoid Burnout & Survive Long Term In Digital Marketing". *Search Engine Journal*, 2019, https://www.searchenginejournal.com/avoid-burnout-digital-marketing/207420/#close.

62. "Know The Signs Of Job Burnout". *Mayo Clinic*, 2019, https://www.mayoclinic.org/healthy-lifestyle/adult-health/in-depth/burnout/art-20046642.

63. Carnegie, Dale. *How to win friends & influence people*. e-artnow, 2017.

64. 2019, https://www.semrush.com/blog/content-marketing-for-millennials-stop-interrupting-and-start-entertaining/

65. Ready, 5 et al. "Paid Media, Earned Media, Owned Media | Titan Growth". *Titan Growth*, 2019, https://www.titangrowth.com/what-is-earned-owned-paid-media-the-difference-explained/.

66. Gallo, Carmine. *Talk like TED: the 9 public-speaking secrets of the world's top minds*. St. Martin's Press, 2014.

67. "What I Learned Watching 150 Hours Of TED Talks". *Harvard Business Review*, 2019, https://hbr.org/2014/04/what-i-learned-watching-150-hours-of-ted-talks.

68. arXiv, Emerging. "By Data-Mining A Vast Collection Of Novels, Researchers Have Identified The Six Basic Plots That All Stories Follow". *MIT Technology Review*, 2019, https://www.technologyreview.com/s/601848/data-mining-reveals-the-six-basic-emotional-arcs-of-storytelling/.

69. Grimaldi, William MA. *Aristotle, Rhetoric: a commentary. 2. Rhetoric II*. Vol. 2. Fordham Univ Press, 1980.

70. White, Graham J. *FDR and the Press*. University of Chicago Press, 1979.

71. Silber, William L. "Why did FDR's bank holiday succeed?." *Economic Policy Review* 15.1 (2009): 19-30.

72. Pfiffner, James P. "Sexual probity and presidential character." *Presidential Studies Quarterly* 28.4 (1998): 881-886.

73. Levy, Sidney J. *Brands, consumers, symbols and research: Sidney J Levy on marketing*. Sage, 1999.

74. Godin, Seth. *All marketers are liars: The power of telling authentic stories in a low-trust world*. Penguin, 2005.

75. Godin, Seth. *This is Marketing: You Can't be Seen Until You Learn to See*. Portfolio, 2018.

76. Berger, Jonah. *Contagious: Why things catch on*. Simon and Schuster, 2016.

77. Schwartz, Barry. "The Paradox Of Choice". *Ted.Com*, 2019, https://www.ted.com/talks/barry_schwartz_on_the_paradox_of_choice.

78. *Amazon.Com*, 2019, https://www.amazon.com/Paradox-Choice-Why-More-Less/dp/149151423X.

79. "Ernestpackaging". *Youtube*, 2019, https://www.youtube.com/channel/UCmZrDgAfbVWuU43i9Krg9fQ.

80. "One, Ten, One Hundred - A Wistia Original Series". *Wistia*, 2019, https://wistia.com/series/one-ten-one-hundred.

81. "4 Reasons Why You Love To Hate Big Businesses". *Investopedia*, 2019, https://www.investopedia.com/financial-edge/0412/4-reasons-why-you-love-to-hate-big-businesses.aspx.

82. "Huffpost Is Now A Part Of Verizon Media". *Huffpost.Com*, 2019, https://www.huffpost.com/entry/millennials-want-brands-t_b_9032718?guccounter=1&guce_referrer=aHR0cHM6Ly93d3cuZ29vZ2xlLmNvbS8&guce_referrer_sig=AQAAAKnIe9GV83t5voCz7-HLuwDK1sNwA9oc6SlG7VT_YynIC0WgcI3GBctZkhd54R9BRXRLgWlifnK6btlg0nOBMPvjJRcl-7CWlB3cwcV_OXoDEKSG6ZB0ZKpoMD1KT0k_PqlI8BpEVu3V2XEoFEeSeGmroZxnZ_v-gdFpaPu2Xg2d.

83. "Watching Film For Basketball: A Scientifically Proven Intellectual Workout?". *By Any Means Basketball*, 2019, http://www.byanymeansbball.com/blog/watching-film-for-basketball-a-scientifically-proven-intellectual-workout.